Action Research in Education

Action Research in Education

Learning Through Practitioner Enquiry

Vivienne Baumfield, Elaine Hall & Kate Wall

Second Edition

Los Angeles | London | New Delhi
Singapore | Washington DC

Los Angeles | London | New Delhi
Singapore | Washington DC

SAGE Publications Ltd
1 Oliver's Yard
55 City Road
London EC1Y 1SP

SAGE Publications Inc.
2455 Teller Road
Thousand Oaks, California 91320

SAGE Publications India Pvt Ltd
B 1/I 1 Mohan Cooperative Industrial Area
Mathura Road
New Delhi 110 044

SAGE Publications Asia-Pacific Pte Ltd
3 Church Street
#10-04 Samsung Hub
Singapore 049483

Editor: Jai Seaman
Assistant editor: Anna Horvai
Production editor: Ian Antcliff
Copyeditor: Jennifer Hinchliffe
Proofreader: Louise Harnby
Marketing manager: Catherine Slinn
Cover design: Jennifer Crisp
Typeset by: C&M Digitals (P) Ltd, Chennai, India
Printed and bound by: CPI Group (UK) Ltd,
Croydon, CR0 4YY

Library of Congress Control Number: 2012947687

British Library Cataloguing in Publication data

A catalogue record for this book is available from
the British Library

ISBN 978-1-4462-0719-2
ISBN 978-1-4462-0720-8 (pbk)

CONTENTS

LIST OF TABLES AND FIGURES

ABOUT THE AUTHORS

Vivienne Baumfield is Professor of Pedagogy, Policy and Innovation in the School of Education, University of Glasgow. Vivienne has been exploring how co-inquiry between teachers, teacher educators and researchers creates knowledge about teaching, for over twenty years. As a member of the Curriculum, Assessment and Pedagogy Educational Reform Group she is currently examining developments across the devolved nations of the UK.

Elaine Hall is Lecturer in Research Methods, School of Education, Communication and Language Sciences, Newcastle University. Working with teachers engaged in practitioner enquiry helped Elaine to recognise that she is simultaneously a learner and a teacher. Her work in professional learning, curriculum, pedagogy and the development of research methods is all connected to the key enquiry question 'What is the experience of the participants – how can they link this with what they have learned and move towards what they want to learn?'

Kate Wall is Senior Lecturer in Education in the School of Education, Durham University. Kate's research interests revolve around the enquiry question, how do participatory methods support authentic conversations about metacognition between teachers and students? Her experience is characterised by collaboration between teaching and research communities. She has strong affiliations to teachers and the role professional enquiry has in supporting learning (for teachers and students). Her approach is a pragmatic one that focuses on mixed methods, using real life examples to explore what works, sharing this across communities to develop better theoretical understanding of the processes involved.

PREFACE

This book is for anyone who wants to find out more about the process of undertaking an enquiry into their professional practice at any stage in their career, from novices to those with many years of experience. We provide an introduction to the key ideas underpinning practitioner enquiry and detailed exploration of processes that are relevant to practitioners in education or other applied fields such as medicine, law, business or social work.

Our approach when working with teachers is to begin with the question, what happens when they engage in enquiry and how do university-based researchers support this process? The framework we provide recognises that a successful enquiry is not simply finding an answer to the original question but one that deepens understanding by throwing up new questions. We take practitioners through the process from the initial intention to undertake an enquiry, through generating the question, exploring what quality looks like, choosing appropriate methods, and being aware of different participants to the analysis, synthesis and dissemination stages. It is not just a 'how to' but also a 'why to' guide.

Recent reviews of the future of teacher education highlight the importance of developing the capacity for practitioner enquiry as an integral part of professional identity, and teachers undertaking a small-scale research project has become commonplace. While this interest from policy makers and regulatory bodies[1] is welcome, the outcomes of teacher engagement in the process of enquiry may not meet expectations if claims to significance are misplaced. Although the number of practical guides for teachers has increased since the publication of the first edition of this book, insufficient attention is given to the need to evaluate the nature of the knowledge created by practitioners.

This 2nd edition of our book extends the focus from teaching and learning in mainstream schools to include further education and higher education contexts. We use a wider range of real life case studies and composite examples drawn from over 15 years of working in the field with partners in

---

[1] The Teaching Agency, Ofsted, the General Teaching Council for Scotland and Her Majesty's Inspectorate of Education (HMIE) have all included practitioner enquiry in recent guidelines for the teaching profession.

schools, colleges and universities to show how they have negotiated the complexities of conducting an enquiry and how they achieve a clear outcome. We have made other changes in this edition to reflect our growing understanding of the power of enquiry to support the transfer of tools and understanding from one educational context to another. Examples of exchanges between such apparently diverse groups as early years practitioners, secondary geography teachers, hairdressing instructors and chemical engineers illustrate how enquiry can promote both intra-professional and interprofessional dialogue. The recommended reading and references sections have also been updated to take account of recent work on practitioner enquiry.

1

UNDERSTANDING PRACTITIONER ENQUIRY

Chapter enquiry questions

- What do we mean by enquiry?
- What is the link between promoting student enquiry in the classroom and teacher enquiry?
- What can we learn across the different contexts for practitioner enquiry?

Introduction

Teachers are problem solvers. The capacity to adapt national policy on curriculum and assessment to meet the needs of the individual learner is at the heart of their professional lives. It is the teacher adept at making adjustments who is effective in tackling systemic problems and who gains most satisfaction from their work (Huberman, 2001; Hattie, 2003). However, the intuitive judgement of individual teachers regarding the 'best fit' of practice to a specific situation can be enhanced through exposure to a wider range of alternatives. This book focuses on how a more sustained, explicit process of enquiry can be developed to promote professional knowledge that is shared by teachers across different contexts. We are university-based researchers who for over fifteen years have worked collaboratively with teachers investigating their practice in the classroom. Our approach is to begin with the question, what happens when teachers engage in enquiry and how can we support this process? The framework we provide recognises that a successful enquiry is not simply finding an answer to the original question but one that deepens understanding by throwing up new questions. The case studies included in each chapter illustrate how teachers across all phases of schooling from the foundation stage to higher education have posed questions, articulated their ideas and tested them. We have tried to convey the sense of improvisation and risk that we believe is an integral part of learning together across different institutional contexts. The book is, therefore, both a practical guide to how an enquiry might be conducted and an attempt to develop a better understanding of the processes and relationships involved.

What do we mean by enquiry?

The literature on professional learning uses a variety of terms, including reflection, enquiry and action research, to describe how teachers try to understand and improve their practice. Sometimes the terms are used interchangeably:

> Teacher research is a type of action research, is synonymous with teacher enquiry, shares many characteristics with practitioner enquiry and incorporates reflective teaching and critical reflective practice. (Lassonde and Israel, 2008: 7)

Although we focus on what the teachers we work with actually do, imprecision in the use of terms can result in a 'lofty rhetoric' (Zeichner and Liston, 1996) and we want to avoid this and try to understand the processes involved.

The term 'reflection' in the context of professional learning is associated with Donald Schön and the term 'reflective practitioner' became very popular after the publication of his books in the 1980s (Schön, 1983; 1987). Schön described the predominant approach to professional learning as 'technical–rational' in its premise that teaching is an instrumental process requiring the application of learned skills in predictable, clearly defined circumstances. He considered this approach to be inadequate to the task of understanding how practitioners make use of intuitive, tacit knowledge and developed his idea of reflection to describe this process. For Schön, reflection is the means by which what would normally be implicit or assumed is brought to the foreground as teachers become conscious of their practice.

Schön describes two types of reflection: reflection-on-action, which takes place away from the event, and reflection-in-action, which takes place in the moment of the event itself. The concept of reflection coincided with common-sense ideas of how teachers think about classroom situations and so had an immediate appeal. The popularity of the term, however, brought its own problems as people began to use it very loosely and it became '… more a metaphor for representing a process of learning from experience than a term that might be subject to more detailed analysis' (Leitch and Day, 2000: 180). Schön admitted that the inconsistent use of the term in his early writings had caused some of this confusion but that the essential characteristic of reflection had always been the emphasis on the importance of an embodied way of understanding practice. The importance of Schön's work in highlighting the significance of the knowledge created by working professionals is beyond doubt. The extent to which the process of reflection, as he describes it, enables practitioners to be proactive in posing problems and drawing upon existing research rather than reacting to issues in the thick of the action in busy classrooms has been questioned. We have found the work of Dewey on enquiry helpful in making these links between reflection, action and learning.

For Dewey, reflective thinking 'impels to enquiry' through the search for knowledge beyond immediate, individual experience (Dewey, 1910: 7). Teachers presented with problematic situations in the classroom look for solutions and collaborate with other people to develop an understanding of what they can do. For Dewey, this willingness to test ideas through experimentation as part of a community of enquirers is indicative of a 'scientific attitude' and marks the continuity between student learning in the classroom and teachers' own professional learning. Focusing on enquiry links directly to teachers' work with their students where the use of questions to stimulate learning is already part of their practice and where it is expected that knowledge will be achieved through dialogue. It is this emphasis on dialogue, with other people and with what is already known, that distinguishes enquiry from reflection.

The term 'action research' was first used by Kurt Lewin to describe 'research that will help the practitioner' by providing clarity about what is to be done in complex situations. The aspiration was to develop an integrated approach to the analysis and evaluation of action through research on particular instances of social problems. Working systematically through a 'circle of planning, action and fact-finding about the result of the action' would result in objective standards for achievement and so facilitate agreement as to the conclusions to be drawn (Lewin, 1946: 34). Action research, along with positive research and interpretive research, forms one of three dominant educational research paradigms (Bassey, 1990) where, despite numerous variations, it retains the universally agreed characteristic of being research designed to improve action. The process of action research involves a series of linked enquiries with teachers formulating questions arising directly from their classroom experiences at each stage in the process. Grundy (1982) developed a typology of action research with three categories: technical action research, practical action research and emancipatory action research. Within the educational research community there has been debate about the scale and scope of action research. In some of its variants the action taken may be modest and the research outcomes not synthesised as completely as Lewin originally envisaged. The extent to which it should be an essentially radical, emancipatory activity is also disputed. The promotion of action research as a form of evidence-informed practice by government agencies such as the Teacher Development Agency (TDA, now the Teaching Agency) has been criticised for limiting its scope. Schemes promoted by the TDA, such as Best Practice Scholarships, were influential in raising awareness of the need for teachers to engage in and with research but risked diminishing the potential of action research by emphasising its technical aspects at the expense of the critique of values intrinsic in practice (Leitch and Day, 2000).

In our work with practitioners across all the phases of formal education, primary school to higher education, we have described the process of investigation as 'practitioner enquiry', which we see as occupying the middle ground between reflection and action research.

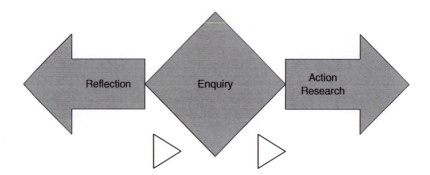

Figure 1.1   Positioning enquiry between reflection and action research

As the diagram above indicates, we think that this middle position can be understood in two ways: practitioner enquiry can be a step in a process that begins with reflection and leads to sustained action research or it can be understood in terms of Dewey's conception of enquiry as the trigger to further development through reflection or action research. In either case, a crucial stage is the forming of questions arising directly from practice and it is the fostering of this intention that we promote through our partnership with teachers. Our approach encourages practitioners to take more account of any existing research that is pertinent to the problem than is the case in most representations of 'reflection'. At the same time, unlike some ideological versions of action research, we are content with a relatively modest focus for an enquiry provided it has arisen directly from practice.

Drawing on our experiences of working with teachers we have constructed an understanding of enquiry that reflects the variety of practice and takes account of the interrelations between three key aspects:

- the intention of the enquiry;
- the process by which the enquiry is pursued;
- the audience with which the enquiry is shared.

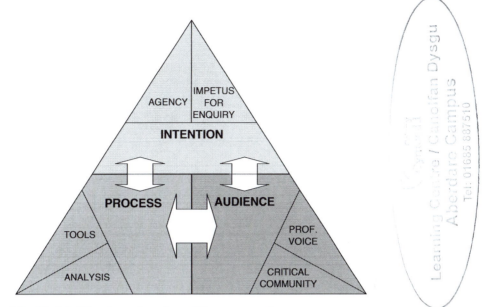

Figure 1.2   Model of the dynamics of practitioner research

Intention

Agency: This refers to the extent to which the individual Teacher-researcher has control of the focus of the enquiry, the methods used to pursue the project, the analysis and interpretation of data and the way in which the project is made public. In some projects other agents such as a senior manager or a university-based research team may control one or more of these elements.

Impetus: The problem posed that stimulates the enquiry and provides the focus for the action research can come from a number of different sources: it can be an issue of concern at an individual teacher level, amongst a group of colleagues, across the whole institution or sector. It can come from an experience in the classroom, from a question posed by an in-service professional development course session, a professional journal or from discussion with colleagues and managers. The impetus for the enquiry will have implications for the processes followed and the primary audience and have an effect on the dynamics of the practitioner research.

Process

Tools: This refers not simply to the research methods employed – the observations, questionnaires, interviews or test scores – but to the extent to which each method provides data which operates on more than one level. A pragmatic research tool simultaneously contributes to answering the research question *and* gives feedback information that enriches the learning and teaching in progress.

Analysis: The analytic process is one in which, broadly speaking, there is either a progressive narrowing of focus to assemble evidence to either prove or disprove a hypothesis or a broad mapping of the data collected in order to generate a rich description and a new hypothesis.

Audience

Professional Voice: Dissemination is a key part of every project, but the extent to which it is prioritised reveals something important about the purpose of the enquiry as identified by the individual researcher. Is the intention to set in motion specific changes in pedagogy and practice, necessitating active dis-semination well beyond the immediate environment, or to set up a ripple effect, whereby the impact of the research is most keenly felt in the immediate vicinity but may spread out through recommendation and colleagues' reports?

Critical Community: This refers not just to the final presentation of results from an enquiry, but how the researcher is placed in relation to oth-ers, from the initial idea, through the process of data collection, re-framing questions and analysing findings. In terms of extremes on the continuum, there is at one end the 'lone' researcher, at the other a formal team with clearly defined roles. However, the points of contact are important less for the number or the length of time, than for the extent to which they both support and challenge the researcher. The standards used to judge the out-comes of research are by no means unproblematic and this is one of the main anxieties of teachers new to research. There are key elements such as clarity, appropriate application of methods selected and ethical considera-tions, which would be expected in any investigation. The role of the com-munity is dynamic, providing an arena in which teacher-researchers feel confident to share their experiences and findings but also one in which they can expect to be asked tough questions. In this way, the quality of research and the learning of individuals and communities are promoted.

In the model in Figure 1.2 we have put intention as the top of the triangle as this emphasises the importance of accessing strategic, reflective thinking in order to consider the meaning of their activity in holistic as well as analytic ways:

> This kind of thinking is important when embarking on activities which make considerable demands on a person, such as an academic or vocational course or project. It can also be extremely valuable in dealing with ... a chal-lenge to an assumption, belief or a communication problem. Most signifi-cantly, it is what changes what could be a routine process into a learning experience. (Moseley et al., 2005: 315)

It is by focusing on the intention of the practitioner research that the impetus of the enquiry and the agency of the teacher are made explicit so that strategic, reflective thinking can be accessed.

What is the link between promoting student enquiry in the classroom and teacher enquiry?

> I've learned a lot from just listening to some of these kids. I'm thinking, WOW, I never figured it out that way.

> Sharing ideas with primary school teachers has had a big impact on how I teach my undergraduate students – that was a surprise for me!

> I learned more from watching the video of one lesson than I did from 25 years in the classroom.

In our work with teachers enquiring into their own practice we have been aware of what has been called the 'mirror effect' (Wikeley, 2000). The mirror effect describes how interventions designed to have a particular impact on student learning have a similar effect on the teachers involved. Our experience of the changes that occur in teachers is corroborated by a systematic review of the impact of thinking skills interventions on teachers (Baumfield and Butterworth, 2005). The review took evidence from 13 empirical, classroom-focused studies covering all phases of compulsory education and across a range of curriculum subjects. All of the studies included used more than one measure of teacher impact as well as data on impact on student achievement so that links could be made between improvements in students' learning and changes in teachers' practice. The studies involved teachers working with their usual classes in normal school settings and so had 'mundane realism' (Coolican, 1996). Focusing on the importance of collaborative enquiry for learning with their students created an appetite for enquiry in the teachers that was marked by a shift in their attention to consider different aspects of the teaching and learning process. The key to this shift was the experience of 'positive dissonance' (Baumfield, 2006) created by the enthusiastic but unexpected responses of their students, which surpassed expectations. It is, therefore, the access to student feedback that triggers teacher interest, stimulates collaborative enquiry and is the basis for growth. The link between student enquiry and teacher enquiry is the enhanced access to student feedback through more sustained, considered dialogue.

Our approach is, therefore, consistent with what is already known from the extensive literature on the importance of feedback for professional learning, which emphasises how teachers themselves can learn from student feedback in the process of bringing about change in classrooms and schools

(Reed and Stoll, 2000; Hargreaves, 2000; Watkins, 2000). Improving access to student feedback may be necessary for teacher enquiry but it may not be sufficient, as researchers in the US have demonstrated. The Cognitively Guided Instruction project (Franke et al., 1998) identified the components needed to facilitate pedagogical enquiry once normal practice has been interrupted by the experience of positive dissonance:

- practical tools
- support for teachers in extending and deepening reflections on experience
- grounding in an emergent pedagogy by having access to a wider critical community
- close collaboration between teachers and researchers.

It is when teachers are able to access support with these components that the meaning-making that enables self-sustaining generative change happens.

This book is about teachers as learners, who by finding out more about what is happening in their classrooms contribute to our understanding of the processes of teaching and learning in schools, further education colleges and universities. It is about developing partnerships in which distinctions between theory and practice are challenged and expertise is distributed as teachers as researchers and researchers as teachers learn together. The relationship between research, policy and practice in the production and deployment of knowledge about teaching and learning is complex and subject to critique (Hammersley, 2005). Nevertheless, conceptions of teaching as a profession assume that a productive relationship between these aspects is both possible and desirable. Our principal concern is to advocate the importance of the research engaged professional; teachers who advance our understanding of the interaction of theory and practice and make a difference to the lives of the students they teach.

What can we learn across the different contexts for practitioner enquiry?

Underlying our approach is the principle of systematic enquiry made public (Stenhouse 1981). The teachers whose case studies inform this book identified questions and initiated changes in their classrooms that were of interest to them and designed an enquiry that was meaningful in their context. The intended audience for this enquiry was characterised as a sceptical colleague who needs to be convinced of the value of the investigation and its outcomes. The enquiries were usually conducted by pairs of teachers situated within a supported network of teachers and university researchers, who operate as co-learners; crucially, the results of the enquiry have to be related meaningfully both within and beyond their immediate context.

Practitioner enquiry has been criticised for the difficulties of generalising results from projects beyond their specific context. While it has high validity for the teacher and the context within which the research was completed, its reliability and transferability can be questioned. This means that the role of partnerships in supporting the teacher-researchers can be crucial. The collaborative nature of enquiry into teaching and learning is important as this helps teachers to develop a professional discourse about learning and provides opportunities for the sharing of ideas across different institutional contexts. Collaboration is a significant aspect of professional development in schools (Cordingley et al., 2003) and this book represents the outcomes from partnerships with teachers in a range of different contexts and over a number of years in which sharing experiences across the different phases of education has stimulated reflection and enquiry into the processes of teaching and learning (Baumfield and Butterworth, 2007). One of the most dramatic examples of this sharing of ideas came about after a residential conference attended by practitioner enquirers from primary schools, secondary schools, FE colleges and a university. During the conference, teachers presented posters illustrating the enquiries that they had been engaged in over the past year and the interest of a Senior Lecturer in Dentistry from the university was captured by a presentation by a primary school teacher about how she had used an enquiry tool called a 'Fortune Line' with her class. He began to wonder if this technique for eliciting the learners' understanding of their own emotions and how other people might feel about a particular event or set of circumstances could help him with a problem he was encountering in his own teaching context. His case study shows how learning was translated across contexts.

Emotional Intelligence in the Learning Environment for Oral Surgery Skills: is managing it a large part of clinical competence?

Undrell Moore

School of Dental Science, Newcastle University

OBJECTIVES

The emotional impact of learning has been recognised as an important element in the design of learning experiences. We have long observed that the act of first removing a tooth has a profound effect on the student dentist as well as the patient. This project sought to explore this in more detail.

(Continued)

(Continued)

HYPOTHESIS

Does reflecting on the experience in 'real time' have an effect on the quality of the reflection and on the students' insight into their learning processes?

RESEARCH PROCESS

In the first pilot study in 2010, 47 students completed an 'exit questionnaire' with standard Likert scales and statements about challenge, emotional experience and new learning. The results from these questionnaires were suggestive but also somewhat 'flat'. They did not represent the intensity of emotional engagement in removing teeth that had been observed during the placement.

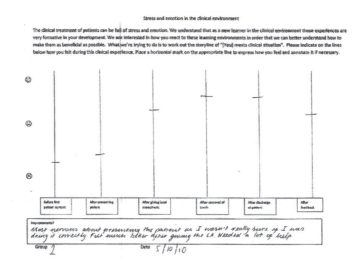

We made the decision in 2011 to use a 'fortune line graph' (above) so that students could record their reactions as each aspect of the extraction process unfolded. All students undertaking the clinical placement were invited to take part.

FINDINGS

Although we have data for a large number of students, for the purposes of this case study an illustrative group of six students is being used.

- Students are more likely to report positive feelings when doing 'hands on' work with the patient.
- Students find preparing for the extraction and receiving feedback on their performance less positive experiences.

- Individual students show significant differences in the small variations of emotional state between activities that [are] also demonstrated in the reflections across the whole placement.
- Tracking student performance and in-depth interviews will allow us to explore whether the emotional experience translates to performance in the longer term.

Group plots

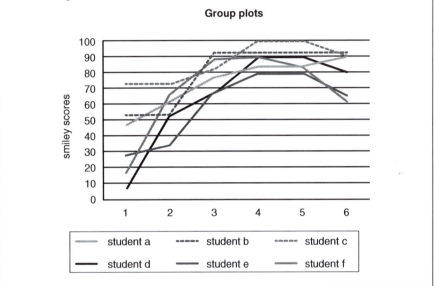

Working across institutional boundaries invigorated the participants as the following comments from a second residential for practitioners engaged in enquiry from primary schools to universities illustrates:

- Knowing about other sectors helps shape your own teaching. It is interesting to learn what is going on in other sectors such as primary and FE when previously there haven't been that many links.
- An enhanced sense of continuity through our practice and consistency (knowing where the students come from and how they were taught – to better address their needs).
- Shared problems, shared solutions, shared community, breaking down perceived barriers, re-energising enthusiasm for learning. Excellent craic!
- We mostly teach the same people, face the same issues (on a pedagogical level) so collaboration should be the rule, rather than the exception.

This book is about teachers as learners, who by finding out more about what is happening in their classrooms contribute to our understanding of the processes of teaching and learning in schools, FE colleges and universities. It is about developing partnerships in which distinctions between theory and practice are challenged and expertise is distributed as teachers as researchers and researchers as teachers learn together. The relationship between research, policy and practice in the production and deployment of knowledge about teaching and learning is complex and subject to critique (Hammersley, 2005). Nevertheless, conceptions of teaching as a profession assume that a productive relationship between these aspects is both possible and desirable. For the teachers, practitioner research is made manageable through the interrelated processes of reflecting on an issue in their classroom, identifying a focus for their enquiry and the generation of a question to be investigated in the classroom. The investigation takes the form of activity that complements the '*plan-do-review*' cycle fundamental to teachers' everyday practice. As such, there is no requirement for the teachers to 'bolt on' or overlay another layer of 'research practices'; rather they select research tools which fit with their teaching environment and use those to generate the necessary feedback in a systematic way. In this model of working it is only a short step from feedback that informs the next stage in the enquiry to evidence that is open to public scrutiny. Our principal concern is to advocate the importance of the research-engaged professional – teachers who advance our understanding of the interaction of theory and practice and make a difference to the lives of the students they teach.

The structure of the book

In this chapter we have discussed the importance of teacher enquiry through a process of practitioner research for understanding pedagogy and improving learning and teaching across different sectors of education. We have outlined a typology exploring the different elements of practitioner research and how they can be configured in different models of the rela- tionship between intention, audience and process. This book will now go on to look at the practical issues of engaging in research into your own practice from the initial identification of a focus to the sharing of your enquiry with a wider audience. In the next chapter we consider the impor- tance of examining the fundamental ideas and assumptions that form your world view as a teacher and how this shapes any enquiry that you under- take. Chapter Three focuses on crystallising a question and making a com- mitment to embark on an enquiry and then the following chapters take you through the stages of an enquiry cycle, giving you practical guidelines, issues to consider and practical examples from the case studies of the teachers with whom we have been working. In Chapter Four we guide you through the process of finding an approach that matches your question and is most likely to generate the evidence you will need to convince more sceptical colleagues. In Chapters Five, Six and Seven we look at who needs to be included in your explorations of issues, from the learners themselves to the wider community. Practical advice is given on how to interest and include other people in your enquiry and how you might consider widening its scope through ongoing enquiry cycles. The final two chapters help you to bring together and make sense of the outcomes of an enquiry and share what you have learned with a wider audience. The book takes you from the forming of an intention to investigate a question to recognising the needs of your audience by showing you what other teachers have done and how they solved problems along the way.

Key readings and References

Key perspectives on enquiry and practitioner research

There is a huge literature exploring enquiry and practitioner research, so the references that follow are intended to be a useful starting point for readers to engage with the debates and the range of views from different traditions.

Dadds, M. (1995) *Passionate Enquiry and School Development. A Story about Action Research*. London: Falmer.

Hammersley, M. (2004) 'Action Research: a contradiction in terms?', *Oxford Review of Education*, 30(2): 165–181.

Hopkins, D. (2002) *A Teacher's Guide to Classroom Research* (3rd edn). Buckingham, Open University Press.

Kemmis, S. and McTaggart, R. (1988) *The Action Research Planner* (3rd edn). Geelong: Deakin University.

McNamara, O. (Ed) (2002) *Becoming an Evidence-based Practitioner*, London: Routledge Falmer.

Menter, I.J., Elliot, D., Hulme, M., Lewin, J. and Lowden, K. (2011) *A Guide to Practitioner Research in Education*. London: Sage.

Somekh, B. (2003) *Theory and Passion in Action Research, Educational Action Research: Special Issue in Celebration of John Elliott's Contribution to Action Research*, 11(2): 247–264.

Whitehead, J. and McNiff, J. (2006) *Action Research Living Theory*. London: Sage.

References used in this chapter

Bassey, M. (1990) 'Creating Education through Research', *Research Intelligence*, Autumn, 40–44.

Baumfield, V. (2006) 'Tools for pedagogical inquiry: the impact of teaching thinking skills on teachers'. *Oxford Review of Education*, 32(2), 185–196.

Baumfield, V.M. and Butterworth, A.M. (2005) *Systematic Review of the evidence for the impact of teaching thinking skills on teachers*. London: EPPI-Centre, Social Science Research Unit, Institute of Education.

Baumfield, V.M. and Butterworth, A.M. (2007) 'Creating and Translating Knowledge about Teaching and Learning in Collaborative School/University Research Partnerships', *Teachers and Teaching: Theory and Practice*, 13(4).

Coolican, H. (1996) *Introduction to Research Methods and Statistics in Psychology.* London: Hodder and Stoughton.

Cordingley, P., Bell, M., Rundell, B. and Evans, D. (2003) *The Impact of Collaborative CPD on Classroom Teaching and Learning.* London: EPPI-Centre, Social Science Research Unit, Institute of Education.

Dewey, J. (1910) *How We Think.* Boston: D.C. Heath and Co.

Franke, M.L., Carpenter, T., Fennema, E., Ansell, E. and Behrend, J. (1998) 'Understanding teachers' self-sustaining generative change in the context of professional development', *Teaching and Teacher Education,* 14(1), 67–80.

Grundy, S. (1982) 'Three Modes of Action Research', *Curriculum Perspectives,* 2(3): 23–34.

Hammersley, M. (2005) 'The Myth of Research Based Practice: the critical case of educational enquiry', *International Journal of Social Research Methodology,* 8(4): 317–330.

Hargreaves, A. (2000) 'Four ages of professionalism and professional learning', *Teachers and Teaching: History and Practice,* 6(2): 151–82.

Hattie, J. (2003) *Teachers make a difference: what is the research evidence? Distinguishing expert teachers from novice and experienced teachers.* Australian Council for Educational Research.

Huberman, M. (2001) 'Networks that alter teaching: Conceptualisations, Exchanges and Experiments', in J. Soler, A. Craft and H. Burgess, *Teacher Development – Exploring Our Own Practice.* London: Paul Chapman, 141–59.

Lassonde, C.A. and Israel, S.E. (2008) *Teachers Taking Action.* Newark DE: International Reading Association.

Leitch, R. and Day, C. (2000) 'Action Research and reflective practice: towards a holistic view', *Educational Action Research,* 8(1): 179–193.

Lewin, K. (1946) 'Action Research and Minority Problems', *Journal of Social Issues* 2(4): 34–46.

Moseley, D., Baumfield, V.M., Higgins, S., Lin, M., Miller, J., Newton, D., Robson, S., Elliott, J. and Gregson, M. (2005) *Frameworks for Thinking.* Cambridge: Cambridge University Press.

Reed, J. and Stoll, L. (2000) 'Promoting organisational learning in schools – the role of feedback', in S. Askew (ed.), *Feedback for Learning.* 127–43. London: Routledge Falmer.

Rodd, J. (2001) *Learning to Learn in Schools: Phase 1 project research report.* London: Campaign for Learning

Schön, D. (1983) *The Reflective Practitioner: How Professionals Think in Action.* New York: Basic Books.

Schön, D. (1987) *Educating the Reflective Practitioner: Towards a New Design for Teaching and Learning in the Professions.* San Francisco: Jossey-Bass.

Stenhouse, L. (1981) 'What counts as research?', *British Journal of Educational Studies,* 29(2): 103–14.

Watkins, C. (2000) 'Feedback between teachers', in S. Askew (ed.), *Feedback for Learning,* 65–80. London: Routledge Falmer.

Wikeley, F. (2000) 'Dissemination of research: a tool for school improvement', *School Leadership and Management,* 18(1): 59–73.

Zeichner, K. and Liston, D. (1996) *Reflective Teaching: An Introduction.* Mahwah, NJ: Erlbaum.

2

WAYS OF BEING A PRACTITIONER ENQUIRER: BELIEFS, ETHICS AND PRACTICE

Chapter enquiry questions

- How do you think truth is generated in education research?
- How does your world view impact on your enquiry?
- What might a good quality practitioner enquiry look like?
- How can ethical guidelines for research be applied to practice?

Introduction

This chapter is focused on helping you to identify your world view and to understand how that will shape any enquiry that you undertake. The chapter sits here – before the 'how to' chapters – because we feel that it is important to get these aspects out of the background. It is too easy to leave our fundamental ideas and assumptions unchallenged, only to find that they have led us to focus on only one aspect of a situation or have encouraged us to ignore any elephants sitting around the room. As you engage with the questions posed in this chapter, you will probably find that things are messier and more complex than you first thought. This is a good thing. The quality of your enquiry will be higher and you will have a more robust ethical awareness. The decisions you go on to make about research questions and research tools will be more realistic and you will be open to a range of interpretations when your data come in.

The impact of your world view

The intent with which you undertake a piece of practitioner enquiry, the purpose, the process and the audience, all depend on your 'real world view'. Your beliefs and understandings about the world will dictate, consciously or unconsciously, the decisions you make at all stages of the practitioner enquiry process. It is the thing that ties it together. It will influence the literature that you like and use, the types of research questions you ask, the tools that you use, the answers you will accept and all the stages in between. By real world view we mean your beliefs about how the world is constructed: how do you decide what is truth (ontology) and how those truths are generated and tested (epistemology).

A useful starting point therefore is to think about assessment, something that we have to deal with every day and also tend to have strong opinions about. You have two pieces of evidence about one learner who is about to enter your class: a standardised test score from an end of year exam and a teacher report. They do not agree: the test score suggests the student has 'got it'; the teacher report suggests that they have not. If forced to choose, which one would you base your teaching decisions on and why? Your decision starts to identify your world view. If you chose the test score then this could suggest that you have a positivist standpoint: you may believe that truths about a learner's ability can be isolated from their context and other influences on their life; that a well-designed test can accurately measure and produce an outcome that can be generalised from; that a well-designed standardised test gives an accurate measure of a child's ability and good basis for making decisions about how their learning needs to proceed. A positivist standpoint draws ideas from the natural sciences. However, if you chose the teacher report then you may tend towards interpretivism. An interpretivist believes it is impossible to isolate variables in the social world and that the context in which they are embedded is important. The interpretivist standpoint argues that the theories of the natural sciences can only be applied cautiously to the social sciences and therefore a report that considers a range of variables and their impact on the learner is more representative of a learner's abilities than a single measure. In this case the view of ability is more complex than a simple number can represent and there is recognition that different things influence it.

We know that this binary opposition is an over-simplification of assessment in practice, but bear with us. If we follow these two themes, teacher assessment versus testing, then we can draw some connections between the ontologies (interpretivism and positivism respectively) and corresponding epistemologies (beliefs about how truths are observed and measured). An interpretivist believes that truths are constructed through social interaction: a learner's attainment is dictated by their experience and interaction with the world and other individuals in it. To truly understand attainment then you need to be inductive and consider multiple sources (is their attainment the same across subjects, across days of the week?) and talk to the individual (are their personal circumstances influencing attainment?). An interpretivist epistemology is often associated with social constructivism, looking beyond the individual to how they relate to their peers, their family, their class and culture, and so on. The context is very important.

On the other hand a positivist believes that some truths can be isolated from the social world. These truths have an existence that is independent of social actors (like gravity or the chemical make-up of the air we breathe, both of which impact on individuals independently of personal or social attributes). This positivist scientific tradition states that we can generate rules and laws based on facts and these can be investigated through experiments that test hypotheses, using a deductive framework. In the assessment example, then the belief is that a well-designed test can generate a score that accurately reflects a learner's attainment regardless of what else might be happening in their lives; it can isolate this test score and treat it as an isolated object, a fact. Once this truth is established then comparisons can be made to other children who have taken the same test and progress over time can be monitored. These assumptions can be seen to underpin school league tables in the UK.

Writing about ontological and epistemological positions has been largely associated with methodology, but they may also influence your choices in life, including the pedagogies you prefer (see the diagram below). By drawing parallels to teaching and learning then we hope to support you in thinking about your preferred methodology.

Hodkinson and MacLeod (2010) have written about this link between pedagogic and methodological positions. They argue that a more positivist individual is more likely to prefer behaviourist learning theory and to use structured approaches of rewards and sanctions in their classroom. These teachers have the core belief that we can reliably predict the behaviour that will result from a certain stimulus if reinforced sufficiently. In contrast, Hodkinson and MacLeod suggest that a more interpretivist individual would be more likely to favour social constructivist learning theories, so favouring more flexible and relational strategies, perhaps including group work and time for children to make sense of, and interpret, the world and better understand their place in it. The core belief is that the range of responses is too wide to be accurately predicted and that norms of behaviour in each group have to develop collaboratively.

There is a further association to this worldview that it is useful to recognise: the nature of the data. So, think about the last empirical (included data) article that you read and really liked, what type of data did it include: numbers, words or both? A piece of interpretivist research, as it is based on the belief that a truth is constructed and dependent on interactions with the context, is likely to rely on qualitative data, which is mostly based on words. Whereas a positivist researcher, who wants to objectify and standardise the world, is likely to rely on measures and therefore use quantitative, number based, data. The real world practitioner enquiry examples below should move these arguments into the classroom context. The first from Aylward High School represents a quantitative, research approach, by secondary

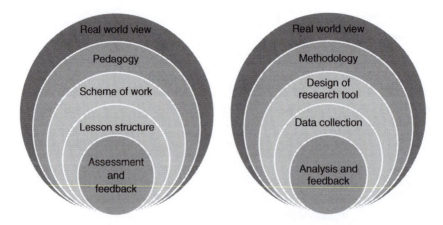

Figure 2.1   'Real world view' supports both pedagogy and methodology

school science teachers with a positivist outlook. The second is a more qualitative approach from Lanner Primary School, representing a more inductive approach to enquiry looking at e-learning logs. As you read through it is possible to see advantages and disadvantages of both approaches. However, at the time when the research was completed, these schools saw these approaches as the most sensible, practical and manageable for them, while also meeting the needs of convincing their target audience.

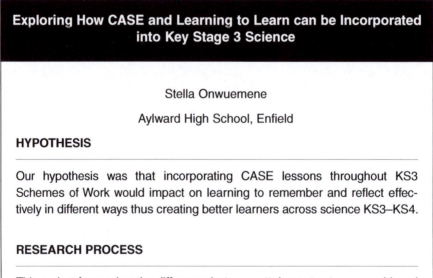

Exploring How CASE and Learning to Learn can be Incorporated into Key Stage 3 Science

Stella Onwuemene

Aylward High School, Enfield

HYPOTHESIS

Our hypothesis was that incorporating CASE lessons throughout KS3 Schemes of Work would impact on learning to remember and reflect effectively in different ways thus creating better learners across science KS3–KS4.

RESEARCH PROCESS

This project focused on the difference between attainment outcomes achieved by each of the three focus classes over the year. Therefore, attainment scores for a variety of different tests dominated the data collected. These included CAT scores and end of topic assessment levels.

FINDINGS

From their CAT scores, the classes appear to be equivalent (see dotted graph below). A one way ANOVA also revealed no significant differences between the classes in terms of original CAT scores.

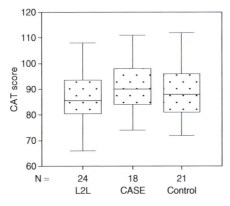

After a year of teaching, the three classes were compared through their members' end of year levels, produced by a SAT type test, and the students' mean levels across three tests. Regressions were also carried out to predict both these outcomes from the CAT scores and the resulting standardised residuals were examined, as measures of gain over the year. The table below shows descriptive statistics for these variables.

A one way ANOVA found no statistically significant differences between most of these means. However the means of the second standardised residual (the end of year level gain from the CAT scores) do vary significantly ($F=3.298$, $p=0.045$) across the classes. The shaded box plots below show the distributions of this standardised residual in the three classes.

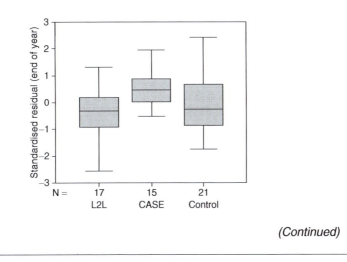

(Continued)

(Continued)

Although the finding of no differences across the other measures of performance should suggest caution, these results do imply that the CASE intervention might improve performance, over either a L2L intervention or no particular intervention. From the box plots, it would seem that the CASE approach might raise the mean performance, but also reduce variation and the tendency for a low-performing tail end of students.

Will Involving Pupils in Reflecting on Learning Through the Use of E-Learning Logs Increase Motivation and Resilience?

Pippa Pender and Liz Martin

Lanner Primary School, Cornwall

HYPOTHESIS

The question we wanted to answer with this research was, will involving pupils in reflecting on their learning increase motivation and resilience?

RESEARCH PROCESS

Evidence was collected from two main sources:

- Children's reflections in their e-learning logs; and
- Teacher's observations

FINDINGS

One aspect of reflection to help learning that came from this project was being able to refer to past learning. Some children managed to use the logs to aid SATs revision by looking back on what they had previously learnt. Work on shape in maths and key words in science [was] used in this way.

It became obvious that the pupils found it difficult to articulate their learning as opposed to what they had done. To help this process a series of questions relating to a reflective journal were displayed in the classroom.

Developing the concepts behind these questions was difficult for most children, even the most able. It was clear that they needed to be introduced earlier, discussed and revisited frequently to make a difference. Probably many of the ideas were too sophisticated to rush through with ten- and eleven-year-olds. In the future the teacher would introduce a few at a time alongside the technology. The whole school approach to assessment for learning also meant that children developed the language and concepts as they progressed through school.

The initial intention to use the logs regularly through the year did not develop as much as the teacher expected. Sad to say, end of Key Stage 2 test preparation got in the way in the summer term. After the tests we recognised (in hindsight) that many opportunities to continue with the logs were missed. Valuable learning experiences of outdoor education, new school visits and school production were missed. However the pupils' responses showed they were beginning to recognise the value of the logs in their learning:

'I like looking back at my slides to remember what we did.'

'I had forgotten about converting fractions to decimals but then I saw them in my log.'

'The laptops help me add in other things and it looks colourful.'

'If I hadn't put the photo in my log I wouldn't have remembered the An Gof tapestry and how good I felt we had done.'

'We did dance with Redruth School and worked together really well as a group.'

CONCLUSIONS

Key findings from the project:

- involving pupils in assessing their own learning increases motivation and self-esteem;
- pupils who use reflection techniques have a more explicit understanding about their teachers' role and themselves as learners; and
- older children in Key Stage 2 appear to be motivated by their success and not by tangible rewards.

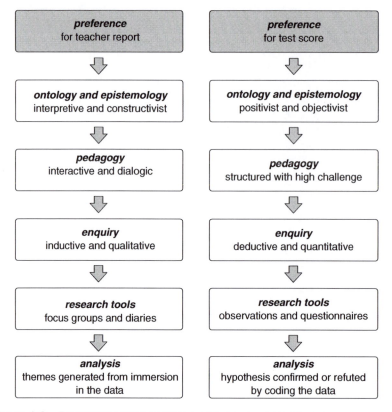

Figure 2.2   Traditional pathways from world view to research process

From this discussion, we could generate pathways from a preference, through world views to the kind of data that might be collected (see Figure 2.2 above) but as soon as we produce something as neat as that we feel compelled to disrupt it. While we are predetermined by our beliefs to ask certain kinds of questions, it is likely that we will be drawn to ask different kinds of questions at different times. This is both influenced by our own preferences and on our awareness of audience: the way in which you might present data about the learners in your class might vary if you were talking to the School Improvement Partner or to their parents. If you are more likely to tell stories at a parent consultation and more likely to have spreadsheets and graphs at your performance review (or indeed, the other way around) this will have an impact on how you notice, collect and organise information in advance of that meeting. When we change the label of your activity to enquiry, you can see how awareness of audience could interact with your preferences to influence the kind of question you ask and the tools and approaches you choose to answer it. It is likely that you will move between positions so we are inviting you to regard positivist and interpretivist as the ends of a continuum of enquiry.

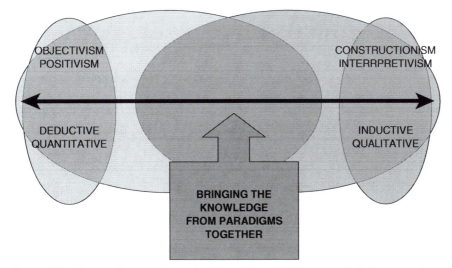

Figure 2.3   The continuum of enquiry approaches and the area of challenge and learning

We get better at doing the things we are most comfortable with when they come into contact with ideas and positions at the edge of our comfort zones. This means that our stories become richer and more convincing to a wider audience when we include the 'who, when, how often, how much' data in the narrative and recognise that a scatterplot of scores and a table of significant correlations can have more impact when a story comes with it. 'Audience' needs to have support and challenge: the ideal is a respect for your ideas and opinions coupled with the permission to ask difficult questions and to disagree, as in a Community of Enquiry, where there is the opportunity to test ideas and self-correct with the support of others (Jackson Wilson, 1968).

The implication, as you've already realised, is that working in this middle zone offers a range of approaches to an enquiry. A mixed methods standpoint (discussed more fully in later chapters) might allow you to make use of tests *and* teacher reports in order to collect convincing evidence from a range of standpoints. However, the question of preferences in terms of evidence is still important: if all your data, quantitative and qualitative, points in the same direction then you might feel that mixing methods has helped you; but if one answers your research question positively and the other negatively, which one are you going to give greater weight to? How are you going to report this messiness and how will that impact on your understanding of your enquiry? Does 'good quality' educational research have more or less mess in it?

Quality in education research

There are a number of facets to quality when considering education research and your view may be different depending on your epistemological standpoint. This includes issues of reliability and validity. However, it also includes ethics, the role of the researcher and the impact or influence of your intent: who is the research for and what is the purpose? There are complex interactions between these elements and we do not intend to explore the wider perspectives here, but rather will focus on ideas important to practitioner enquiry approaches. We think that reflecting on these concepts is important because they are often forgotten about within a research design or are left as implicit because they are felt to correspond to an established epistemological standpoint – 'that's the way we do things round here'. Too often they are given cursory attention when the value of the research process comes from the awareness with which it is undertaken (the intent), the awareness of the intended audience and the degree of fit between this understanding and the tools and approaches used.

Reliability and validity

The terms reliability, validity and generalisability, are all closely tied up in the research process. Reliability is the extent to which the study can be repeated and the same results achieved. Reliability is often cited as one of the key characteristics of positivist research design; for example, the standardised test is designed to accurately measure the achievement across learners, across geographical locations and, in some cases, across time and get an equivalent result that supports comparisons. However, the reliability of interpretivist research approaches is also important, particularly given the emphasis on context. Imagine, for example, a study in which all the teachers in a school gave reflective interviews during March about their professional lives, their beliefs in their pedagogy and their sense of how effective they were as educators. The school is inspected on March 10th and a very critical report published on March 18th. Could we consider the interviews to be a reliable instrument and compare those done at the end of the month with those at the beginning or with those that took place between the inspection and the report? So important questions you need to ask are whether the measure is consistent and is it stable across the occasions in which it is used? Reliability is closely linked to replicability; could someone else re-run your research and get the same results?

In practical terms this means that if you are developing a data collection tool, then you need to think about the wording of questions/instructions and make them clear and unambiguous. Is the language accessible to all and are questions/instructions going to be understood in the same way by all respondents? Will the categories for observation be applied consistently over time and in different subjects and contexts? Are the processes for administering tests being adhered to? Once the data is collected you need to ask whether, during analysis, are you being consistent in your processing of the data; when you are coding, are you consistent over time (intra-rater reliability); or if you are collaborating, is there consistency between coders (inter-rater reliability)? We can all make errors of measurement, even when using reliable tools (as anyone who has tried to make a soufflé will testify) but it becomes even more complex when we start to move towards more subjective judgements: for example, if you are measuring attendance and a student turns up half way through the lesson then are they coded as absent or present? Are you consistent in that decision over time?

In a research project looking at questioning behaviours in classrooms, observers were asked to note open and closed questions and two things happened to make this apparently simple task more complicated. Firstly, some of the researchers decided that an open question depended on the apparent intent of the teacher, while others decided that an open question could be determined by the variety of responses to it. This means that the same question – *'What do people think about that?'* – would only be coded open by both groups if a range of responses came back from the learners, whereas if they all came back with a 'safe' similar response, or no response, it would be coded closed by the second group. This difference in coding only became apparent to the team as a whole because of the second phenomenon, which is that as you use a coding system, you tend to question it and your ideas. Some of the 'teacher intent' group started to adapt their definitions and some of the 'group response' coders did too, and they started to discuss this at team meetings. You can make your own judgements about the reliability of the whole set of observations and, suffice it to say, a whole lot of re-coding had to be done. Of course, some of the observers found their beliefs reinforced by the coding process, which illustrates the benefits of working in a team, so long as you don't mind complexity.

This subjectivity obviously increases as you use tools that require interpretation of words or pictures either as a prompt at data collection, as part of the analysis process or both. Thinking about how to increase reliability across this interpretative data is difficult, but it does not make it redundant as it has other advantages.

If reliability is the principal concern of the positivist researcher then validity is often cited as the preoccupation of the interpretivist: 'validity is concerned with the integrity of the conclusions' (Bryman 2003: 30). In other words, how well do the findings fit with the research questions asked and the process undertaken – do they ring true? There are a number of types of validity that it is useful to consider: ecological, external, internal and measurement validity. For the practitioner enquirer, ecological validity is particularly important as it relates to the extent to which the research findings fit with the context in which the research is set. This is particularly important if research is to influence practice. The findings need to have relevance to teachers and to be true to the world that they recognise if they are to influence teaching and learning.

A valid research tool fits well into the learning environment under examination and measures change using terms that are understood and valued within the context. So if you are completing research with young children then undertaking a standardised literacy test might not be appropriate as the children's reading skills are insufficiently developed and any response would need to be mediated through an adult; an alternative might be to use a visual prompt and response. This fits well with the nature of the target respondents (has ecological validity), but it increases the subjective factor. Validity can be increased however by an iterative process whereby feedback loops are built into the data collection procedure. For example, if collecting data about school to college transfer then you might undertake a series of interviews with the students; to ensure that your interpretations of the data are valid and fit with the students' understandings, then you could feed back your findings at intervals in the process, perhaps using them to design a later interview. In this way you ensure that your findings truly reflect the attitudes and beliefs of your respondents (see Figure 2.4). Of course the disadvantage of this is that you are decreasing the reliability as you are increasing the validity. You have to decide how to balance the two in your research design – which do you value as a sign of quality in your research?

Rigour and warrant

Rigour and warrant are fundamental ideas for assessing the quality of research and they are strongly related to one another. Rigour refers to the extent to which a piece of research meets the requirements of its paradigm: a good positivist study will have ensured the balance and neutrality of the sampling and the way in which participants are assigned to intervention or control groups; it will have employed measures with acceptable levels of

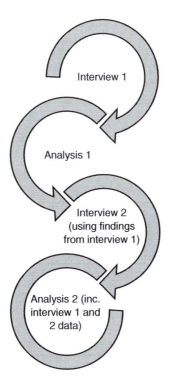

Figure 2.4   Increasing validity: feedback loops within data collection and analysis

reliability and construct validity; the analysis will use appropriate tests (rather than pressing every button on the statistics software and crossing one's fingers for a significant result). It will not be judged to be a bad study because it did not provide open-ended opportunities for participants to interact and challenge the research questions, use methods that encourage the development of narratives or because it did not take account of socio-cultural nuances, since these are criteria by which interpretivist studies are judged. Evaluating research from within its context is an important philo-sophical position for practitioner-researchers, because we need different kinds of knowledge and this allows us to know 'what it is by what it does': a positivist study can tell us by how much students' maths scores and motiva-tion to do maths homework changed after an intervention, while an interpre-tivist study can tell us which aspects of the intervention staff and students believed were the key levers for change.

If a study has been designed and conducted to a good enough standard according to its lights then we can take the evidence from that study and begin to consider the warrant. Warrant refers to the weight that the practitioner can place on that evidence when taking a step forward or choosing to stand in place. A rigorously performed study gives reasonable warrant for starting a new action or sticking with an established one; a less rigorously performed study needs the support of other studies in order to bear our weight securely. This is one of the advantages of systematic review and meta-analysis, since small, imperfect studies, that in themselves don't give warrant, can be part of a larger project of gathering evidence. John Hattie's (2010) book *Visible Learning* is the best resource for exploring meta-analysis and offers some challenge to accepted ideas of 'what works'. Warrant doesn't just relate to the quality of the study, however; it is also related to the context of the enquirer: what I need to know; the degree of fit between the study and my circumstances; the timeliness of the evidence to the phase of my action. A fantastic study on the design of curriculum for talk in the early years has little warrant for me if my issue is managing talk within a highly prescribed set of experiences with adult learners; I might put greater weight on a less rigorously solid article which focuses on *either* a more similar group *or* working with a set curriculum *or* something more descriptive about the way in which talk happens in the micro-interactions of learning relationships. The only way to be really clear about warrant is to discuss how evidence has been selected and used, to accept that context and preference interact with seemingly more objective ideas of quality.

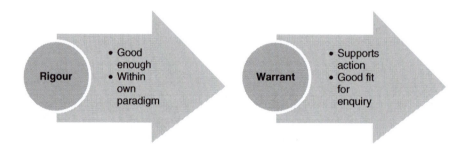

Figure 2.5   Comparing rigour and warrant in practitioner enquiry

The role of the researcher

The positioning of the researcher in relation to the research process is relevant when ensuring quality because of the associations it has to the real world views identified above. From an objectivist's perspective the researcher should minimise his influence so as not to add variables or prejudice the results (the researcher in a white coat is a good metaphor for this position). In contrast, as constructivists believe the truth is generated through social interaction then the researcher cannot be distanced from the research process as his beliefs will be fundamental in generating and interpreting the data and as such should be recognised and embraced. However, this can lead to the same oppositional positioning discussed above. In addition, with practitioner enquiry, where a teacher is researching her own practice it might appear to be a moot point as they are inherently involved. However, a teacher might strive to make relatively little impact: for example teaching the same lesson to three matched classes which differs only in one key element – the way in which the learners are grouped – in order to try to isolate the effects of that element. This is a reasonably objectivist approach, dependent upon the teacher having normal access to separate groups of learners, since if the teacher had worked with unfamiliar classes, there would have been confounding effects from this. Many practitioner enquiries are driven by a specific problem in a class or an exciting new pedagogical idea that the teacher has discovered for themselves. Under those circumstances, this more experimental approach isn't such a good fit, since the teacher isn't neutrally observing various effects; she is passionately interested and invested in a positive outcome from a particular intervention. This does not mean that the research will be invalid but it does mean that the impact of the teacher's enthusiasm and commitment becomes part of the study, so an interpretivist approach allows this to be written about and analysed. In thinking about the intent of your enquiry and the resulting process it's absolutely vital for you to be transparent about your role and how it might impact on the process and findings.

One of the key questions here is the balancing act between pedagogy and research. As a practitioner enquirer you are involved in both. Wherever possible the two should interlink and complement, with tools supporting the outcomes of both, with research findings influencing pedagogy and pedagogical reflections impacting on the research process. As will be discussed in the next section, Groundwater-Smith and Mockler (2007) state that this relationship is an ethical requirement of practitioner research. However, one of the crunch points which could emerge is how you are going to deal with a change in teaching and learning part way through the research process. This could be because of outside influence, for example an unexpected inspection, or it could be directly related to the research with an unexpected result meaning that a change of practice is necessary. Do you stop the research and change the teaching or do you see the research through? This is where the practitioner overrides the researcher.

One way that this positioning can become apparent is the way that research is written up. A piece of research where the role of the researcher has been as a distanced observer tends to be written in the third person, whereas the researcher who is embedded in the context under examination might write in the first person, including their own reflections and interpretations directly. There is no right or wrong position to take, but if you are talking about influence on your own practice then writing about this from a third person perspective can become difficult.

Reflections of Assessment to Promote Attainment

Jillian Rees

Early Years Department, Northumberland College

HYPOTHESIS

Can regular use of a reflective cycle improve student attainment in summative assessments?

RESEARCH PROCESS

The study took place with a group of 18 Level 3 childcare trainees (aged 16–21). Fortnightly personalised learning sessions were used to engage learners in structured reflection. A comparable course group was used as a control group. The process took place over four months during which learners had the opportunity to upgrade one assessment and submit then resubmit a further two).

The focus group undertook an L2L course and was then introduced to a reflection cycle and given a format to support this (see below). Learners tend to be disappointed with their assessment results therefore it was hoped that undertaking a cycle of reflection would enable the learners to tackle any feelings of disappointment and channel them into preparation for a resubmission (thereby developing resilience and readiness).

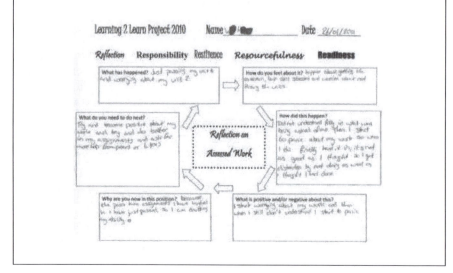

The research was not smooth sailing. One of the learners' assessments was impacted upon by severe weather. They were not prepared for their assessment, having failed to complete prerequisite requirements. A progress review format (see below) was therefore introduced to encourage reflection.

Additionally, limited interactions in the focus group during reflection sessions were felt to be having a detrimental effect. In response, a case study (based on observations of the focus group) was presented as a reflective exercise, challenging them to analyse needs and action plan a response. The intention was to support the group to apply resilience and utilise reflection to improve their teaching and learning experience. When considering the case study, however, over half of the learners were unable to identify that it was about them!

CONCLUSIONS

Observations indicated varying levels of engagement and ability with reflection. Some learners, although initially reticent, became more engaged and capable. For example,

> I do not understand fully what is being asked of me then I start to panic about my work so when I do finally hand it in; it's not as good as I thought so I get disheartened by not doing as well as I thought I had done.

Others began the process enthusiastically but then began to invest less in their reflections, taking less time and care over the process.

(Continued)

(Continued)

It is clear that while a learner's achievement can be quantified as a grade, their journey cannot and reflections by learners in this project indicate they felt this was equally, if not more, important. While the project set out to improve student ownership of assessment work thereby improving grades, ultimately it identified other factors such as limited interaction that seemingly had affected attendance, retention and achievement.

However from experience we know that some practitioner enquirers, often from the more positivist end of the spectrum, find it very difficult to put themselves in the centre of their research and write using I. Whether first or third person, we encourage you to include your own personal reflections, even as part of an objectivist design, as your practice is fundamentally at the root and as such cannot be ignored, however distanced your research design allows you to be from individual data collection tool processes.

Ethics

Previous debates about practitioner research ethics have tended to focus on the difference in perspective between teachers and university research ethics procedures, which are based largely on experimental research traditions, require considerable administrative process and are tied directly into funding and accountability. A useful discussion of the issues that arise from the university perspective can be found in Hammersley (2009). It is not possible (as it once was) for university researchers to recruit people to research projects without telling them the purposes of the research, without assessing the potential impacts of taking part and allowing people to make informed consent about their participation. In schools and colleges, however, the learners are expected to participate in any reasonable activity that the teachers suggest. As practitioner enquiry becomes ever more widespread, with a close association of the research to practice, the real life context and the position of the researcher (in the school and in the research process), a university style of ethics and consent feels alien and difficult to manage. However, practitioner enquiry is not the same as 'normal' teaching and learning and the focus on ethics in this chapter is intended to make us all look again at the practice that we take for granted. The discomfort that arises from this is important; it is this 'positive dissonance' (Baumfield, 2006) that enables us to learn new things about our work and the opportunities for change.

It has been established that classrooms are multi-faceted and extremely complex; therefore the ethical considerations relating to researching it can be equally intricate and subtle. This ethics section will therefore explore the ethical considerations that should be intrinsic to any research design, both in conception and administration, focusing on the 'costs/benefits ratio': finding a balance between thorough investigation and the privacy of their subjects (Cohen and Manion, 1998). We will also spend some time discussing the ethical considerations surrounding the involvement of learners in research as this is likely to be an important aspect of many enquiries. However we will also focus on the ethical positioning of the teacher in regard to their enquiry and its relationship to practice.

The British Education Research Association (BERA, 2004) offers a set of principles and advice that can support the aim of ethical research. The box below gives an overview of these guidelines. These headings will be considered in turn in regards to a practitioner enquiry through action research approach.

The Association [BERA] considers that all education research should be conducted with an ethic of respect for:

- The person
- Knowledge
- Democratic values
- The quality of education research
- Academic freedom

The person

Academics used to talk about 'research subjects': that's not considered polite nowadays, so we talk about 'participants'. It is important that this shift is about more than language, however, or we are continuing to use people in a way that we would object to being used ourselves. There are key questions to be asked and we urge you to shift your position when considering your study and to ask yourself how you would experience it.

- What is it like to be a participant in a research project?
- Why might someone agree to take part?
- What might encourage you to join in and what might make you cautious?
- What information would you need at different points in the process and what opportunities would you like to change your mind about taking part?
- What right of reply would you want in publications about the research?

Knowledge

'Voluntary informed consent' is a key term here and it is important to emphasise that the extent to which something is genuinely voluntary depends upon there being enough clear information. If you recruit me (as a parent) to a study about children's homework practices, I need to know what I'm going to be doing, what measures or research tools are going to be used, and how often and how that data will be published. If I'm going to keep a homework diary, for example, I need to know whether scans of pages from it are going to be used to illustrate the report that will be on the school's website, if only so that I use my best handwriting.

In the case of children it is essential that consent is obtained not only from the parents, which as teachers tends to be one of our first considerations, but also from the children themselves. If you are researching children's perspectives or behaviour then you need to inform them about the intention of your research (in accordance with Articles 12 and 13 of the United Nations Convention on the Rights of the Child, 1989) and also the role that they are going to play within it. If you are asking their opinion then it is important that you do not deceive them, that they know why and how the research will be done and that they are able to drop out if they wish at any stage.

Democratic values

With regard to teacher research, you have to think about how you treat all people, whatever their age, sex and background, directly and indirectly involved in the research. This is hard because as a teacher you are likely to be used to being in control; for example, we have often spoken to teachers who are thinking about recording pupil talk without their knowledge. As teachers we do this as we assess progress, but in research, particularly when you are intending to making the findings public, then you have to consider whether it is appropriate and ethical. To get accurate and ethical results you need to make sure individuals give informed consent and understand what you are enquiring about. These points are important with children, but they should not be forgotten when working with adults as well.

In addition to thinking about consent, you also need to think about whether incentives are appropriate – a good bribe can work a treat with young children and grown up children alike – but you need to use common sense as to the appropriateness of what you are offering and whether using incentives will impact on the outcomes of the research. For example, a prize draw for all completed questionnaires returned by parents will go a long way to improving return rates and it should not impact on the answers given as a draw does not rely on the answers given.

The quality of education research

High quality research has several key factors: the intent of the researcher is clear, their methods and analysis are a good fit for the question and they report the research accurately and in enough detail for any reader to assess whether or not they can place any confidence in the results. Any research with human beings that does not report how people were recruited, what information they were given and what opportunities there were for feeding back to the researchers or for leaving the project cannot be called high quality. If you state clearly how you have framed your enquiry with your participants then you have achieved a level of quality that is sadly missing from a lot of work published in prestigious academic journals.

Academic freedom

We have previously mentioned that a part of the systematic enquiry approach we are suggesting is the making public of any findings. When you do disseminate your findings the privacy of your participants must be assured and they must be reassured of this right from the beginning: you would not want to give your honest opinion of how your school is run if there was a chance that your potentially controversial thoughts might be traced back. It is important that you give participants the right to confidentiality and this should stretch to how you store the data as well as how you report your research. You cannot, in the era of the internet, promise anonymity to your participants but you can take care not to identify individuals: scans of learners' work can be cropped to exclude their names; classes can be given codes rather than the names or numbers used in the school; a quote can be attributed to 'a senior teacher' rather than 'the head of geography'.

The final aspect which we believe makes for good ethical research is the closure of the feedback loop. To show that you are genuine about the contributions made by your participants, whether time taken to talk to you, to filling in your questionnaire or to allowing access to teaching and learning, you need to make a commitment to feeding back your findings to them. With the student voice agenda currently prevalent in schools, students are being asked more and more regularly for their opinions, but very rarely are the findings and indeed the resulting actions taken on their behalf fed back. We believe that this is really important for fulfilling the BERA ethical guidelines (2004).

Of course this commitment to closing the feedback loop and ensuring that the participants have a say in how the data collected from them is considered, interpreted and reported means that you are asking them to invest in the process and outcomes, and, quite likely, as a result give time to their production. There is an argument here that if there is a co-production of knowledge, all contributors should be credited and by anonymising half of the team that produced this thinking you are being unethical. Indeed in the examples used in this book, we have explicitly credited the teachers and organisations that have undertaken enquiry with us; it is their work that is reported here and so they deserve equal recognition to us in the production of the resulting knowledge. Of course, to take this kind of approach permissions need to be sought and feedback loops need to be tight so that the individuals concerned can see and comment on the way that their work is being represented, but we feel that this is worth it and the ethically sound way of recognising the partnership that made the work a successful learning experience.

Recently, the American Educational Research Association has published new ethical guidance (AERA, 2011). It makes the connection between the practice ethics of the teacher and the research ethics of the enquirer much more explicit:

> It is the individual responsibility of each education researcher to aspire to the highest possible standards of conduct in research, teaching, practice and service.

> Adhering to a set of ethical standards for an education researcher's work-related conduct requires a personal commitment to a lifelong effort to act ethically; to encourage ethical behavior by students, supervisors, supervisees, employers, employees, and colleagues; and to consult with others as needed concerning ethical problems. Each education researcher supplements, but does not violate, the values and rules specified in the ethical standards based on guidance drawn from personal values, culture, and experience.

This appears to us to be a much more inclusive and empowering view of ethical practice and we would encourage you to consider how congruent your personal, professional and research ethics might be by asking on each occasion, 'Would this be OK if it happened in my personal life, in my teaching practice *and* in my research project?'

Therefore there are two aspects to considering ethics and practitioner enquiry. There is Groundwater-Smith and Mockler's position that the imperative to undertake quality practitioner enquiry is ethical in its very nature,

> ... that the dynamic that exists between practitioner research and professional practice for educators is such that ethicality cannot be divorced from quality in professional practice. (2007, p. 209)

Secondly there are the ethical considerations within each stage of the research process: the iterative processes of examining ethical principles in design, recruitment, engagement in the process, control over the data and contribution to interpretation and dissemination. The principles of ethical practice inform pedagogy and enquiry.

Key readings and References

AERA (2011) 'Code of Ethics', *American Education Researcher*, 40(3): 145–156. Available at: http://www.aera.net/AboutAERA/KeyPrograms/SocialJustice/ResearchEthics/tabid/10957/Default.aspx

Baumfield, V.M. (2006) 'Tools for Pedagogical Inquiry: the impact of teaching thinking skills on teachers', *Oxford Review of Education,* 32 (2): 185–196.

BERA (2004) *Revised Ethical Guidelines for Educational Research*, BERA. Available at: www.bera.ac.uk/files/2008/09/ethica1.pdf (accessed 18th August 2011).

Bryman, A. (2003) *Social Research Methods*. Oxford: Oxford University Press.

Cohen, L. and Manion, L. (1998) *Research Methods in Education* (4th edn). London: Routledge.

Groundwater-Smith, S. and Mockler, N. (2007) 'Ethics in practitioner research: an issue of quality', *Research Papers in Education*, 22 (2): 199–211.

Hammersley, M. (2009) 'Against the ethicists: on the evils of ethical regulation', *International Journal of Social Research Methodology*, 12 (3): 211–225.

Hattie, J. (2010) *Visible Learning*. London: Routledge.

Hodkinson, P. and Macleod, F. (2010) 'Contrasting concepts of learning and contrasting research methodologies: affinities and bias', *British Educational Research Journal*, 36 (2): 173–189.

Jackson Wilson, R. (1968) 'C.S Peirce: the Community of Inquiry', in R. Jackson Wilson (ed.), *In Quest of Community: Social Philosophy in the United States 1860–1920*, pp. 32–59.

United Nations Convention on the Rights of the Child (1989) *UN General Assembly Resolution 44/25*. Available online at: http://www2.ohchr.org/english/law/crc.htm (accessed 28th January 2010).

3

HOW TO DO A PRACTITIONER ENQUIRY: FINDING AND REFINING A QUESTION

Chapter enquiry questions

- How can you get from an idea or a hunch to an enquiry question?
- What is a good enquiry question?
- Has somebody else already answered this question?
- How can you make your enquiry manageable?

Introduction

We began this chapter in the first edition with 'Once convinced of the benefit of enquiry and the action research cycle for learning about the teaching and learning process in your context, the next stage is to focus on which aspect you want to explore, what questions you want to ask, what change you are expecting and how you are going to measure/observe that change'. However, feedback suggests that some readers start here (rather than with chapter 1) with a niggling sense that something might warrant investigating, but are not yet convinced about exactly how this might be done. This chapter has been re-shaped, therefore, to offer support to the phase of crystallising a question and making a commitment to embarking on an enquiry. Chapter 4 then picks up the crucial decision-making process of research design and the choice of research tools.

The stone in your shoe

We suspect that there will be something within the context of the classroom in which you work which is bothering you. Something is going on that you don't quite understand: a teaching approach is working much better than you'd expected, or not working so well with a particular group of learners, or you have new technology and you're not sure exactly what kind of impact it is having. You will have these 'professional musings' quite often but some of these questions become more pressing; you become more aware of them as a constant presence, things that you'd really like to pull out of your shoe and take a closer look at.

> I would like to improve ...
> I want to change ... because
> I am perplexed by ...
> Some people are unhappy about ...
> I'm really curious about ...
> I want to learn more about ...
> An idea I would like to try out in my class is ...
> I think ... would really make a difference to ...
> Something I would like to do is ...
> I'm particularly interested in ...

Figure 3.1   Starting points for enquiry

A key consideration is that it is *your* stone: the problem is right there in front of you, driven by your context and your learners and intimately bound up with their needs. You might find the question 'Which is the best way to improve access to the secondary history curriculum?' interesting in a general way but when you have Billy, who has access issues, in your class then it becomes imperative. This means that we have a series of ethical commitments bound up in the purpose of our research (Groundwater-Smith and Mockler, 2007). Our research needs to provide information we can use, for our school development, for our own and our colleagues' professional learning and to improve the experience of our learners.

As practitioner-researchers, our starting point needs to be turned into a question that is answerable and manageable. Broadly, there are two types of enquiry question: '*What's going on?*' and '*What happens if?*' A practitioner enquirer needs to decide whether they are investigating an existing phenomenon (what's going on?) or whether they are going to instigate a change and explore the impact (what happens if?). Often cycles of enquiry move backwards and forwards between these two types of question. A teacher might start with a new approach to teaching reading and have a 'what happens if?' cycle of trying it out in class, followed by a 'what's going on?' cycle of looking at how the skills the learners demonstrated in reading transfer (or don't) to other areas of learning. Alternatively, the teacher might start with a 'what's going on?' cycle when they know something is not going right but are finding it difficult to isolate what needs to change in order to decide which intervention would be the best bet. This process is exemplified in Table 3.1, which looks at the following enquiry question: *why doesn't the group-work part of my lessons work that well?*

Table 3.1   Moving to an enquiry question

Starting point *Why doesn't the group-work part of my lessons work that well?*

What's going on?	**Aspect of practice**	**Measure**	**Enquiry question**
	How are the groups in my class organised?	Mapping the classroom	In group work, is there any variation in performance between
	Do some groups appear to be working better than others?	On task/off task observations	
	Does that impact on their performance?	Assessment of work	• different groups? • observed behaviour and outcomes?
	Does this change depending on the nature of the task, the time of day or other factors?	Repeated observations and assessment over time	• different tasks? • other factors?
Depending on the results of the above, we ask – What happens if I?	**Aspect of practice**	**Measure**	**Enquiry question**
	Change the way the groups are constituted?	Experimental design?	Does working in a self-selected group improve performance?
	Make the kind of task more collaborative?	Enquiry tasks developing over time?	Does group work need a real question to be effective?
	Change the nature of the assessment?	Make success dependent on the type of participation: talk, management, recording?	Can I assess process as well as outcome in group work?
	Restrict group work to specific times in the day/week/term/module?	Reflect with colleagues on the place of group work in subject or age/stage pedagogy?	What is the purpose of group work in my subject and how can I make it more effective?

Either type of question is equally valid, but the distinction is important as it will influence the kind of answer that you are looking for and therefore the process that is undertaken. Once this decision is made, then the next stage is to think about the aspect of practice that you are interested in and how it could be measured or observed (the evidence you might collect). This information can then be combined to support the development of your question, making sure that it is a realistic one which can be answered within your context.

For an enquiry to be fruitful then it is important that the area of research is closely related to your own experience as a teacher. Enquiry needs to be owned by the teachers who are completing the work and it needs to be located within their own domain as practitioners. In our experience, unproductive research tends to be focused away from the practice and context of the Teacher-researcher and this means that the teacher does not feel sufficiently motivated and involved to see the research to its conclusion. Successful research also tends to involve 'action'. In other words, there needs to be some kind of translation or development of knowledge and understanding for the teacher for the research to feel effective. This could be a change in practice or a change in the learning environment, or it could be a validation of existing practice, but it is likely in either case that there will be further questions and hunches to be explored.

Once you have conceived an idea or hunch for your enquiry, then you need to start framing your thoughts into a question. Now this can appear easier than it is, because the important aspect of this question is that it has to be answerable. That is achievable in terms of the data that it is possible to collect, the measurability of the outcomes and the data collection tools available and practical for use.

The first stage is defining the elements which might change as a result of implementing the change/innovation that you are interested in. So for example, if you think that an approach such as Mind Mapping will support the pupils in their learning, you need to think about how this will be manifested. Will students demonstrate improved learning and, by that, do you mean better understanding shown in talk or classroom processes or higher attainment in tests? It is likely that students will be able to produce better Mind Maps, though you may want to reflect on what your criteria are for a 'better' Mind Map.

The second stage is to think about what this change will be, what it will look like and therefore how it can be evidenced: you may think there will be observable changes in all of these areas as a direct result of implementing the Mind Map technique. You might therefore want to capture pupils' talk to see if they are displaying better curriculum knowledge in tasks, either in peer or plenary discussions. You will be monitoring their marks in tests and coursework as part of normal practice but this also 'counts' as research data. Once you have decided on your developmental framework for Mind Mapping, you can assess whether students demonstrate a linear progression or whether particular elements of the course lend themselves more readily to this approach. However, the complexity of analysing *both* audio recordings and Mind Maps might be too much in terms of workload, so you will have to make choices about which changes you are most interested in. In this way the focus of your research becomes more specific and therefore more answerable.

It will probably be apparent by now that there will not be one single way to undertake an enquiry, but throughout this reflective process you will be continually slimming down your focus and you can begin to ensure that your question is *answerable*. The next stage is to consider whether the question that you proposed is *manageable*. Firstly, whether what you are proposing fits into your workload and into your teaching week or year and secondly, whether your research question is a good fit for the complexity of teaching and learning in your context.

Manageability: your workload

There is a fantastic creative phase to an enquiry when you start to see endless possibilities for data collection and innovative ways to analyse that data. This can be followed by an 'out of control' feeling if you do not take time to reconcile the research tasks that you are giving yourself with your workload as a teacher. This is therefore the next element which is essential to making sure that your research is manageable. From our experience this is not a difficult process but means that you need to plan out your research tasks alongside school commitments on a chart, such as the one below. This chart is for the school year. Your research might be over a period of time shorter or longer than this. You just need to adapt the timescale to fit.

This chart aims to allow you to plan out your research and make sure that it fits with the school year. So for example, if you are a primary school teacher whose class is involved in the school nativity play every year, then to do any data collection in the run-up to Christmas might not be appropriate: firstly, the children will be high as kites and therefore any data collected might not be representative, and secondly, if you are involved in rehearsals then your time is going to be pressured and any research is likely to suffer.

When	Project tasks	Other school commitments
Term 1 Sept–Oct		
Nov–Dec		
	Christmas	
Term 2 Jan–Feb		
Mar–April		
	Easter	
Term 3 April–May		
June–July		

Figure 3.2   Planning tool

The same type of thinking might surround a secondary teacher during exam time (both mock and actual), when pupils might be difficult to catch as they are on study leave and there is disruption to the timetable, which can leave very little spare time. These types of events however can be planned around as they tend to be at fixed or predictable times and the research therefore can be timetabled accordingly.

This process of consideration should support you in being confident that the question is manageable and that it is answerable. This is a necessary balancing act between the evidence which can be collected and the pressures of a teacher's daily/annual routine. The two need to be reconciled as much as possible.

Manageability: making your question a good fit

The contexts in which we need to undertake research in education, however large or small, from nationwide evaluations to the examination of one to one exchanges, are complex and impacted upon by a huge variety of variables. It is almost impossible to cut out and eliminate all of these variables without putting the teacher and their class in a laboratory – which we do not want to do.

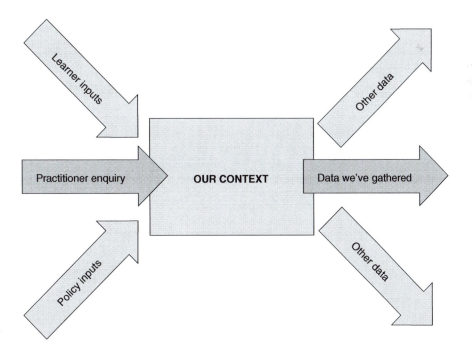

Figure 3.3   Thinking about the influence of variables on every teaching and learning context

A visual representation of the problem can be seen in Figure 3.3. As a researcher you want to be confident that you are getting the right answer to your question and that there are the minimum number of possible influences which could affect this answer. In other words, you want to be sure that your research design is making as close a link between the input (your innovation/change) and the output (the identified change) as possible, with little interference as from associated and impacting variables along the way. You may try to limit the number of other variables that could have an impact on your enquiry but overall it is reasonable to accept that you are not going to be able to do your research in sterile laboratory conditions. What you can do is be very clear about what you think are interesting variables (what you are going to look at) and what you think are less interesting/too hard to capture/less relevant variables (what you're not going to focus on) and why. One of the disadvantages of collecting more than one type of evidence is that while trying to give the process more clarity and making the associations between inputs and outputs more convincing, the manageability of the actual process may be reduced. An aspect of manageability is the precision of the research question. This means wording the question in a way that is unambiguous (for example, instead of saying '*improve attainment*' use '*raise marks from a mean of 65% to 80% in end of module tests*') and reasonable (is an increase of 65% to 85% realistic, either within the timescale set or given other learners' attainment in the same test?). We also need to ensure that we are only asking one question, or at least that we have unpacked the elements within our question. This is illustrated with another example of an enquiry question in Figure 3.4, below).

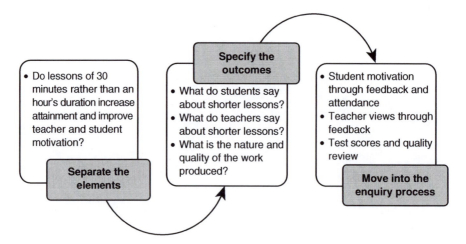

Figure 3.4   Unpacking the elements in an enquiry question

One of the ways to do that is to look at what other people have already done.

Is the truth 'out there'?

There is an awful lot of research about teaching and learning. It is published in journals, in research reports, in government materials to support practitioners, collected in books, summarised on websites and featured in professional magazines. If you started now and did nothing else but read research until the end of your life you could still not keep pace with what is being produced and you would have no time for the day job. For this reason – and with some justification – many teachers are a bit wary of engaging with research. It all seems too much. However, there is a lot of pressure on teachers to be 'research-informed' and to be able to say what the evidence is for their practice, so in this section we focus on some of the key skills needed by teachers to engage with academic papers, research reports and policy documents.

What's out there and how to make sense of it

It's particularly important in the age of information overload to be able to make well-informed choices about the things we read. If you google 'effective group work strategies' (as we did in October 2011 and got 71 million hits) then you will get a rich mixture of books, articles, blogs, advertisements, courses, policy discussions and exhortations, people selling their books, articles and courses and so on. The first level of sorting is to get rid of the people telling you what to do and focus on those people who are sharing what they have done. Adding 'research', 'study' and 'empirical' to your search terms is a good idea, as is narrowing the field to your age group or subject area to give you a smaller group to start with ('effective group work strategy empirical research study secondary geography' takes the hits down to five and a half million, for example). Many of these people will have some actual data and you will then be able to engage with their work and decide whether you think it is relevant, well designed and worthy of your attention.

One of the principal issues about accessing information from the internet is quality control. Anyone can upload content and being able to design a professional-looking site does not guarantee the quality of what is posted. Sites that are managed by or affiliated to universities, professional organisations and governments may be of a higher quality but it is still likely that the document that you download is the product of a small group or an individual's thinking and that it has not been subject to critical scrutiny. The 'gold standard' therefore remains the peer-reviewed journal article, since in this process work is submitted anonymously, judged on its own merits by experienced people in the field and frequently improved in the light of their comments.

Getting hold of peer-reviewed research studies can be an issue for teachers in schools. There are some open-access sites and these are growing but publishers and journals understandably want to make money from their material. The reality is that a lot of what is free is 'teaser' material, intended to draw the reader in and encourage them to buy, so trying to get hold of free high quality material can be frustrating. As an individual, it may be worth considering the old adages about false economies (especially given how 'time-poor' most teachers feel) and consider either setting aside a budget for downloading material from academic journals or investing in an access card that will allow you to use your nearest university library. If you can persuade your school to be in an active research partnership with your friendly local university, then that is what we (all based in universities) would shamelessly recommend as the best option.

How to read research

Once you've got hold of your document you want to be able to do four key things:

- establish what data it contains and whether it is relevant
- assess the quality of that data
- make the connection to your own context and questions
- fillet out any new references

If you are reading a journal article, it will probably have an abstract; if it is a research report, there may well be an Executive Summary and this can be invaluable in helping you to make a quick decision whether to read the whole document. However, there is a problem in that many abstracts and summaries do not accurately represent what is inside. Please complain to the authors when this happens to you, as this is the only way it will get any better!

There is a temptation to read the article or document front to back but we would caution you against this when looking for evidence to support or challenge your enquiry. The traditional structure of academic writing is for the author to provide their theoretical and philosophical background before getting to the nitty-gritty of the study. If the study participants turn out to be too different from your own learners or the intervention used is very different from the one you plan to use, you will have spent quite a lot of time getting to know the author before you realise that you won't be spending much more time together. For this reason, we recommend the reading equivalent of speed-dating: have some key questions that you get answers to in the first five minutes. To do this, you need to find the section where the paper or report describes what was done – often under the heading of *methods* or *design*. The checklist below gives some key points to look for: if you aren't happy with the number of ticks you can give the paper, it's probably not worth you engaging with the author's reflections and conclusions.

Key questions   ✓

Who took part in this study?

Are details given of age, gender, ability, special needs, socio-economic status, ethnicity and culture?

Are details given of how they were recruited, what ethical steps were taken and who dropped out?

Were the participants in their normal setting, working with their usual teacher?

What outcomes were investigated?

Was the focus on:

- attainment (knowledge, skills, understanding),
- attitude (to the content, to the process, to the self as learner),
- behaviour (increase in positive or decrease in negative),
- or a combination?

How were the outcomes measured?

Who designed the measures?

If there were questionnaires, interviews or observations, were the instruments included for you to see?

If there was an intervention, was there 'before' and 'after' data?

If views were gathered, was the sample large and representative enough?

How were the data analysed?

- If numbers, does it state which tests were used and give you enough detail to check it?
- If words, does it explain how the themes were generated and how the words were placed within the themes?

Figure 3.5   Research method checklist

The absence of something from this list does not make it a bad paper but it does allow you to ask key critical questions and to develop a quality-controlled list. If you read a paper that says that it is telling you what learners experience in a particular situation but it does not tell you how these learners were recruited and what rights they had to withdraw, then it carries less weight than a paper which includes those details. A study that uses some open-ended research methods to ensure that all views can emerge is likely to be more valid than one that uses only a closed-response questionnaire designed back in the office before the fieldwork took place. A paper that goes on to explain how the analysis of learners' views was then fed back to the learners to be checked gets even more points, since we can start to feel confident that the authors have been rigorous in checking out their ideas.

Once you have started a collection of papers, you can begin to arrange them in terms of how good you think their evidence is based on your checklist and, in a lovely feedback loop, you can be checking out how valid and rigorous your research question is in the light of what other people have done.

Making decisions about warrant

Overall, the purpose of 'engaging with' the literature is to develop your own enquiry, so that you can begin 'engaging in' as well (Hall, 2009). The professional in search of support from the literature for her enquiry doesn't have to start by browsing the research shelves, selecting one paper and asking, 'How might this work in my classroom?' As craftspeople, teachers may explore how well a mass-produced solution will address their own problems and, on finding it less than adequate, may instead consider producing something for themselves: a bespoke, tailored resolution. However, given the time and effort involved, there remains a tension for teachers between privileging their contextual expertise and the risk of re-inventing the wheel.

> [E]ducational research, as opposed to simply research on education, will involve teachers in its construction and execution and not simply in applying its findings. Teachers engage in educational research and not simply with it'. (Elliott, 2001; 565, emphasis in original)

What we are suggesting is that your critical engagement allows you to make 'good enough' decisions about actions, changes and enquiries in your teaching. You might not know everything but you have a reasonable understanding of how much weight you can place on various bits of the evidence map that you have created from your reading and research. This gives you the confidence and backing to move forward; this is your 'warrant' (Dewey, 1938). Chapter 4 will now take you through the process of choosing how to do this.

Key perspectives on research design

Bryman, A. (2008) Social Research Methods (3rd edn). Oxford: Oxford University Press.

Cohen, L., Manion, L. and Morrison, K. (2011) Research Methods in Education (7th edn). London: Routledge.

Denscombe, M. (2003) The Good Research Guide (2nd edn). Berkshire: Open University Press.

Lewis, I. and Munn, P. (1997) *So You Want to Do Research! A Guide for Beginners on How to Formulate Research Questions.* SCRE Publication No. 136. SCRE: Edinburgh.

References used in this chapter

Dewey, J. (1938) *Logic: The Theory of Inquiry.* New York, NY: Henry Holt.

Elliott, J. (2001) 'Making Evidence-based Practice Educational', *British Educational Research Journal*, 27(5): 555–574.

Groundwater-Smith, S. and Mockler, N. (2007) 'Ethics in practitioner research: an issue of quality', *Research Papers in Education*, 22(2): 199–211.

Hall, E. (2009) 'Engaging in and engaging with research: teacher inquiry and development', *Teachers and Teaching: Theory and Practice*, 15(6): 669–682.

4

HOW TO DO A PRACTITIONER ENQUIRY: DECIDING ON AN APPROACH AND COMPLEMENTARY METHODS

Chapter enquiry questions

- How can you choose the best data collection tools to answer your research question?
- What constitutes evidence and how can it be collected?
- How can mixing methods provide new insight to your enquiry questions?
- How can your enquiry convince a sceptical colleague?

Introduction

In Chapter 2 we asked you to reflect on your own beliefs about the purpose of education research, what quality looks like and how this fits with ethical considerations, from both the research world and education. Then in Chapter 3 we outlined how you should develop your enquiry questions ensuring they were realistic and answerable. We encouraged consideration of what you want to find out and how to therefore pose the enquiry question and how different types of enquiry can inform each other. This chapter will now put all of this theorising into practice and will turn your attention to how you are going to collect data. We will explore what constitutes data, how to be critical about approaches and what best answers your research question.

Convincing a sceptical colleague

It is important to think about who you want to convince with your evidence. In other words, who will be your potential audience for your study? This could be colleagues within your school, the senior management team, peers at Local Authority level or a wider community of enquirers. You will need to decide and think about this as you frame your research design and think about the evidence that it's best to collect to convince your chosen audience.

In addition to choosing the potential audience, we have then found it helpful in research projects to have teachers think of the most potentially sceptical individual in that group and to use them as the target for at least a couple of the evidence sources. We believe it is possible to identify such an individual in most groups and if not then a fictional individual with these characteristics might be appropriate. The quote below from a teacher involved in action research exemplifies this process.

Action research has proved a very useful tool for supporting the implementation of new ideas and practices in our school. When we were first presented with the idea of action research both my partner researcher and I were interested in its power to persuade reluctant colleagues to have a go at new ideas.

We felt that if we had some kind of proof about the power of the techniques we were employing with the children, other staff would be more motivated to have a go at it themselves. We were right. The fact that our first year of research did not provide us with much quantitative evidence proved unimportant with the rest of the staff. They were most excited, as we had been, by the qualitative findings from the pupil views templates. They were so excited about what children had to say about their learning and the vast difference between the views of the 'Paired Learning' and the control class, that ten out of the fifteen classes wanted to trial it for themselves. (Primary school)

There are so many different data types which you can think about collecting that it is important to sift through which are the most appropriate to your own interests, to your context and to your intended audience. Over the next couple of sections we will outline the different types of evidence you might think about collecting. As you read through these different ideas it could get overwhelming. We have a broad view of what data can be collected as evidence and in addition we will suggest a range of individuals who could be consulted about the impact of change. Therefore we propose that while bearing in mind the manageability aspect, you always keep in mind the evidence you would use to convince this sceptical colleague.

Different types of data

In social sciences there are two main types of data. These are:

- **Qualitative data:** tend to be word based, for example, transcribed interviews
- **Quantitative data:** tend to be number based, for example, test scores

As highlighted in Chapter 2, researchers tend to ally themselves with one or the other of these types and the epistemological and ontological standpoints that they represent. So for example, some might say they are more convinced by quantitative data, which means that statistical significance should be looked for as the benchmark of impact; whereas others might argue that this type of number-based data does not give the detail of why that significance was achieved and so rich qualitative description and explanation are of more value. Indeed a split can be seen within the education system itself, with policy makers tending towards more quantitative impact (for example, the A*–C pass rates, attainment) and teachers often being more interested in qualitative data (for example, positive beliefs and attitudes, achievement). This reflects a historical divide over what makes good research and is summed up by the natural science versus social science debate.

As a broad rule, we tend to see quantitative data as telling you *what* happened on a specific occasion and qualitative data exploring *why* that might have occurred. Examples of each type of data that might be used to explore impact on learners can be seen in Table 4.1 below.

Table 4.1   Contrasting qualitative and quantitative evidence

	QUANTITATIVE	QUALITATIVE
Learners' attainment	Test scores	Interviews
	Teachers' marks	Logs/diaries
	Examples of work	Examples of work
Learners' attitudes	Questionnaire	Interviews
	Survey	Logs/diaries
	Observation/video	Observation/video

Rather than continue to promote this dichotomy we would encourage you to think of it as a flexible relationship between the two elements. Yes, there are researchers who would subscribe to one view or another, but there are others who take a more eclectic approach to their research design, trying to mix and match the best of both worlds. We argue that you need to think about your audience and apply these types of data accordingly. For example, if your intended audience is policy makers at LA level then you might prioritise SATs or GCSE results and attendance figures as a likely prime concern of these individuals, whereas if your audience is other teachers then test scores might be important, but they could also be interested in the attitudes of the learners and the impact on classroom behaviour that the change brought. In other words, in a very pragmatic way such a study might tend to want to explore whether there was a rise in attainment, but also to check whether there was any impact on classroom ethos and atmosphere. In such an example, a method that includes both quantitative (what happened) and qualitative (why it occurred) might be more appropriate. This could be argued to be more meaningful, since as teachers we want to know about the 'what *and* why' because we are always striving to move forward in our practice.

What constitutes evidence?

In the previous section, we introduced some of the different types of evidence considered by researchers in universities and research institutions and we have given examples as to how this data might be collected in schools. However, we need to consider the role of the Teacher-researcher. A teacher has access to different types of evidence that might not be considered by, or may not even be available to, researchers from outside of the school. Using these sources of evidence can support you in balancing your research with your teaching and learning commitments.

Education as a field of practice is data rich and the majority of teachers are skilled and experienced evidence collectors. So in addition to the traditional social science techniques, the Practitioner-researcher can consider their normal routine and the vast number of ways that data is collected each day, term, or academic year to explore admissions, progression, retention and success. This means that as long as you are answering your research questions and the data is meaningful in doing this, then most sources can be construed as evidence. Therefore we would encourage you to be as inventive and as expansive as possible in considering what data collection tools you are going to use in your own research. The following categories of potential evidence should be useful in this thinking:

- **Traditional research methods** – This category includes interviews, questionnaires and observations, all of which are extremely useful in both a quantitative or qualitative research strategy. However you might like to think about how they can be adapted and used so that they fit with the agendas behind some of the categories below.
- **Data collected normally in schools** – Schools are data-rich environments: data are being collected at individual pupil/teacher level, at class level and at school level all the time – for example, Individual Education Plan (IEP) records,

attendance, behaviour logs and test scores. This type of data does not add much to your workload to collect and has the advantage of often large and consistent data sets across the school.

- **Data arising from teaching and learning activities** – Teachers are always asking different individuals, especially pupils, to do different activities. This category therefore asks whether these outputs can be used as part of your research; for example, work samples and learning logs can be used to tell the story of a child or a group of children's learning over the period of a term or school year. Yes, these are being collected specifically for the research, but they are adding a new element to your practice related to learning and teaching.
- **Data collection that can be incorporated into school routine** – Given that accountability and self-evaluation are current themes within education, there are various techniques which can be built into this framework and can be part of your research while also fulfilling other elements of a teacher's job. For example, peer observations can be focused around research-based observation schedules and the pupils' school council can be used to survey opinions of the student body.

So for a Teacher-researcher there is a broad range of resources that can be tapped into, but this can feel overwhelming. A critical edge is needed when considering what constitutes good evidence in the context of your enquiry; it is important that some strategic thought is applied to how these data might provide additional insight and contribute in answering your enquiry question.

One of the key practical messages that we want to get across here is that ideally evidence should be collected, where possible, to fulfil more than one purpose. This helps with the manageability of the research process. So, if the register is being taken at the start of a class every session, then this data can be used for your research to explore whether pupils' motivation to turn up to your new and improved lessons has manifested in better attendance. If pupils are completing learning logs to aid their reflection on learning across subjects, then ask the students if it is OK for you to look through and identify whether they perceive that they learn more when you use the specific innovation you are interested in. If your research design needs observations to look at teacher behaviours, can you incorporate it into the teaching staff's routine peer observations?

The table below uses example research questions and explores the types of data that could be collected using our four categories of evidence. This is in no way an exhaustive list and there are many other ways in which evidence could be collected and included; indeed the teachers whose questions these were chose different methods again (talked about in the next section). However, the aim is to get you thinking not only about the broad range of data available to you as a teacher, but also about how you can combine the two roles of teacher and researcher to make the process as manageable as possible.

Table 4.2 Thinking about different types of evidence and how they can answer your research question

Question	Traditional research method	Data collected normally in schools	Data arising from teaching and learning	Data that can be incorporated into school routine
Will boys' attainment in writing (using teacher assessments) improve after using peer assessment?	Questionnaire to pupils to explore their perceptions of their learning and improvement in writing before and after peer assessment.	SATs and complementary teacher assessments collected over the year and then compared to a mean achieved by previous year groups.	Work samples from the group of target boys, collected on a per-term basis, to look at the improvement over the year. Both teacher and pupil give comment as to how this improvement manifests itself.	SMT observations of peer-assessment lessons focusing on target pupils and their approaches to writing-based tasks.
Does the use of visual cues support the improvement of behaviour for pupils with AS disorders in whole class sessions?	Interviews with the pupils' teacher and support staff exploring any perceived changes in behaviour and improvements in attention related to the use of cues.	Individual pupil observations, an element of each individual pupils' IEP, which look at different behaviours and how often they occur – do lessons where visual cues are used reveal different/improved behaviour?	Using a sorting activity based on a favourite book: can the pupils complete the task better when visual cues are added? Look at the pupil outcomes as well as the teacher perceptions.	Incorporating the capture and analysis of video footage of pupils in whole class situations into support assistants' routine for monitoring individual pupils' behaviours and for logging inappropriate behaviours.
Will using more open questions in class discussions improve the on-task behaviour of all pupils?	Structured observations of the pupils' contributions and behaviour in lessons where open questions are used and when not (could be based on video footage). Looking at on-task/off-task behaviour and length of utterance from pupils.	Logs of negative and positive behaviour, e.g. how many merits achieved or how many sanctions administered within each lesson. Does it improve when open questioning approaches are in use?	Using a thinking skills activity, e.g. a mystery, investigate whether the pupil–pupil discussion and the outcome is different in a class where open questions are used when compared to when not. Look for pupil use of open questions.	School-wide system of pupil observations exploring what makes a good lesson and what makes pupils engage with the curriculum content and with discussions. Findings fed back to whole school, teaching staff and pupils.

Across our work with teachers we have been amazed at how teachers and schools have either gathered research evidence from existing school routines and structures or have adapted and changed these same routines to fit with the needs of the research. In most cases all agree that this development process of balancing research evidence and traditional teaching and learning evidence has been a positive experience for the teachers involved and for the school as a whole.

A new type of data? Visual methods

Having stated that there are two types of data, qualitative and quantitative, we are now going to somewhat controversially introduce a third type, visual data. Visual methods are not new, although they have been relatively rare in comparison to words and numbers; however, in the last 20 years there has been a rapid increase in their use in the social sciences. In education this increase can be linked to the UN Convention on the Rights of the Child and the need to find ways of communicating effectively with children and young people about their experiences of school. This means the use of visual data has strong links to pupil voice and participatory research traditions but its growth has additionally been fuelled by new technologies that have opened up the way it can be collected, stored and accessed. Digital cameras, for example, have revolutionised the ease with which photographs can be taken, displayed and edited for a range of purposes.

Visual data includes all types of visual communication including photographs, drawings, signs, symbols, video, diagrams, cartoons, paintings and patterns (for examples see Figure 4.1). Prosser (2007) argues for three categories of visual data:

- the visual element is part of the data collection tool design (researcher generated);
- it is generated as part of the data collection process (participant generated); or
- it is the data itself (researcher found).

In our experience teacher-researchers are particularly good at seeing the potential for incorporating visual elements into the research process. This should be no surprise considering the way that visual data is used every day in classrooms across sectors as prompts, stimuli for discussion or as ways of interrogating thinking; although arguably this does decrease as students get older. This acceptance of visual data tends to mean that teacher-researchers are more creative with Prosser's categories. For example drawings completed by a Year 1 class on the theme of school (researcher found) might be analysed for common themes representing children's perceptions. This analysis and example pictures could then be used as researcher generated data to collect

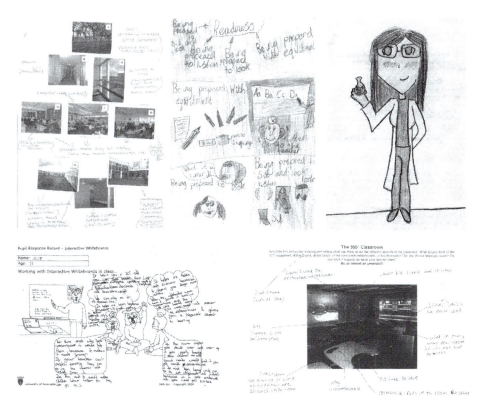

Figure 4.1   Examples of visual data

parents' perceptions allowing for a comparison of attitudes. Therefore there is a blurring of Prosser's categories because a single piece of data can fulfil the operate in multiple categories across the research process. We do not see this as a negative, but it is important when using visual approaches to be critical about the purpose with which you are using the data and the objectives that you want it to fulfil.

The example below from Lewisham FE College incorporates the visual element as part of a participant generated activity that aimed to explore students' study skills. Diamond ranking was chosen as it fulfils similar purposes to traditional techniques such as an attitude questionnaire: to systematically elicit respondents' beliefs. The visual element, the structure into which the statements had to be sorted, was chosen to be more motivating for the respondents and to add a dimension of fun to the data collection exercise. It was rationalised that this technique was different enough to increase the response rate and the authenticity of the answers. It aimed to stimulate conversation between the students so as to ensure thought around the topic area, an objective that might have been achieved through the use of focus groups, but within the more economic and structured parameters of a survey. Indeed, a ranking activity such as this might be expected on a traditional questionnaire. But the diamond meant that the ranking process was more flexible in accommodating the complexity with which teachers tended to view learning and teaching, while keeping to a format that allowed an analysis procedure that enabled comparisons.

The Impact of 'Study Skills' on Metacognitive Knowledge and Skills

Pele Mobaolorunduro, Geoff Davison, Mo Pamplin & Dean Britton

School of Health, Care and Early Years & Learning Services,
Lewisham College

PROJECT AIMS

The stated aims of the project were to investigate students' confidence and competence in using study skills (abstract skills in thinking, planning and organising knowledge), which, together with an awareness of when these skills should be used and the individual's knowledge of his or her competence in the various skills, can be categorised as metacognitive knowledge and skills – that is, thinking about thinking: students' ability to think about and evaluate their own thinking skills.

RESEARCH PROCESS

The study involved working with a group of 30–45 college students from the school of Health, Care and Early Years, as they attended a summer school run by lecturers from the school in July and August 2009. This summer school is run every year. A number of different research activities were implemented during the course of the summer school, focusing on allowing the students to discuss and compare their studying strategies, habits and attitudes to learning.

In one of the activities students were required to diamond rank (see diagram below) their confidence and familiarity with the following skills areas:

- Note taking
- Understanding the main point of a piece of writing
- Time management
- Using other people's work
- Taking the time to plan
- Academic writing style
- Using and understanding new words

- Proof reading
- Writing a bibliography
- Critical awareness of research sources
- Reading quickly
- Number, maths and statistics

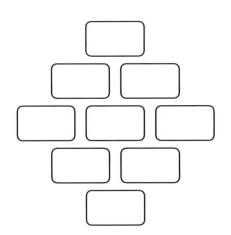

FINDINGS

Of the twelve skill areas given, *note taking* scored the highest in terms of students' confidence and familiarity; *understanding the main point of a piece of writing* and *time management* also received higher scores. *Number, maths and statistics* attracted the lowest scores.

These results were achieved by reviewing the diamond ranking activity the students completed, which asked them to rank twelve skill areas in terms of their confidence, familiarity and competence in these areas. We gave a score of 5 to the single skill placed on the top row; 4 to the two skills in row 2; 3 to the three in row 3; 2 to the three in row 4; 1 to the two in the bottom to last row; and 0 to the skill ranked at the bottom. We extracted the mean and modal score for each skill. Both averages placed the skills in very similar ranking positions, with the two extremes unaffected.

Further isolated analysis of this result was resisted, since the students had completed the activity in random groups, and several of the skill areas allowed for interpretation of meaning.

We have one health warning to attach to the use of visual data, and we speak from experience. It is very easy to get carried away collecting visual data. It is very easy to do especially when working with young children. It is easy to collect thousands of digital images or hundreds of children's drawings relatively economically, which is good when you are working full time, but these sample sizes can feel overwhelming. There is a great complexity in the depth and breadth of each individual piece of visual data and the way it is incorporated (or not) into the research adds further variables. Images are constant and lasting; they are easy to store and revisit and this means they are open-ended and almost boundless in the level of interpretation that can be applied over time. In addition, individual texts can be used in connection with other pieces to fulfil different purposes. This can be relatively small scale, for example an exploration of commonality between two drawings by the same child; or it could involve the examination of a sample of images taken at one time to investigate a specific idea across respondents; or it could be a comparison of data sets to evaluate an intervention. These different designs open up new challenges. Depending on the intent of the text and the way in which it is being used, then the extent to which the breadth and depth of each individual text can be considered has to be seen in relation to the sample as a whole. As a Practitioner-researcher you need to make sure that you are clear about why you are collecting visual data and therefore how it will be analysed and how many individual texts will be needed to fulfil this purpose.

The rise in visual approaches is exciting and has enabled investigations into new and different contexts (for example, gathering perceptions from young children or from individuals with communication impairments) and allowed new light to be shed on old debates (for example, new ways of understanding metacognitive development). We encourage you to think about the visual evidence you can collect in your enquiry and not limit yourself to just words and numbers.

Thinking about the data collection process: participatory methods

As stated above visual methods have been linked to participatory research approaches, but this is a larger and increasingly important category within education research more generally. Participatory methods emphasise participation of respondents in the collection, synthesis and/or analysis of data and crucially the power for the research process is less with the researcher and more equally distributed across all those involved. So instead of doing research *to* a target population, you do it *with* them.

In the case study below we have outlined a participatory approach that was undertaken in an enquiry focused on international students' understandings of assessment in a higher education institution. Here the Practitioner-researcher shared her enquiry question with the students and was transparent about the intended learning for herself (pedagogic understanding of how to introduce and use formative assessment with international students) and the students (better understanding of assessment and its use in a UK university). Ultimately the students and the teacher took co-enquiry roles.

Participatory approaches have advantages and disadvantages. The main advantages lie with the bottom-up nature of the research, the transparent standpoint on issues related to power and the management of ethical issues encompassing voice and ownership of the research and its outputs. And to be honest, the criticisms lie along similar themes: it is argued that it will be inherently impressionistic and biased due to the involvement of the subjects, and unreliable because of the range and level of involvement. In the end, your uptake of a participatory approach will depend on the intent of your enquiry and the type of questions you are asking.

Within a practitioner-enquiry framework, where intent is centred on improving learning, then participatory approaches often seem a sensible way forwards. If you are exploring a new pedagogic technique in the classroom, for example not using PowerPoint in a postgraduate seminar, then being honest about what you are trying, and involving the students in evaluating progress, means that not only do you get quick feedback but it also opens up discussions about what works in teaching and learning and can support outcomes. We believe it is a good thing for teachers to admit they are learning too! The disadvantage of being this transparent is that from a traditional research perspective you are adding in variables and impacting on the reliability of the research. If the students know about your enquiry, will this bias their responses in some way? Only you can decide whether the potential outcomes, benefits to their learning, outweigh any potential influence on the data.

What is Assessment?
Do Our Understandings Match with Students'?

Victoria Rafferty
INTO, Newcastle University

RESEARCH QUESTION

What is assessment: do our understandings match with our students'?

(Continued)

(Continued)

CONTEXT

INTO Newcastle University is currently in the third academic year of operation and is a partnership between INTO, providers of International Education, and Newcastle University. The Humanities' programme is available for international students who have not qualified for direct entry onto one of many Social Science-related undergraduate degrees. It is skills-based, meaning that specific knowledge is secondary to the primary intention of providing opportunities to develop crucial skills, such as formalised writing.

RESEARCH PROCESS

The anticipated benefits were that students' semester 1 grades will be higher than those of their previous counterparts. Secondly, that the current students will have a greater understanding of formalised writing. All 23 students of mixed nationality were included.

During week 1 the students were asked to construct a concept map, by annotating an A3 sheet with the word 'assessment' on it, with their ideas of what assessment meant to them. For four weeks the students attended compulsory, taught, one-hour sessions aimed at academic essay writing process and conventions. At the end of each session, the students were asked to complete a reflection based on the question 'what information will you use to help you with your current assignments?'

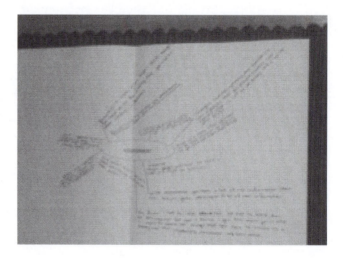

After the final session, the students were asked to reflect not only on that session, but also on the 4 sessions together, based on the questions 'What have you learnt about the requirements of assessments at this level? Have you changed anything about your writing from how you might have written an essay before you came onto the programme?'

This overall reflection was to allow students to think more holistically about their writing. The students were also asked to consider their initial concept maps and amend if necessary. Any changes, it can be argued, could provide basic measurable data as to whether changes in thinking about assessment had occurred. I was also interested in the language used on the concept maps, and in the reflections, providing qualitative information about conceptions of assessment.

CONCLUSIONS

Colleagues believe the intervention is a positive addition to the programme. In a recent focus group, to inform module evaluations, the *assessment sessions* were commended by students for being helpful in aiding understanding of the requirements of essays. This information will be available to the programme's External Verifier.

Using mixed methods

It might be apparent by now that we are steering you towards collecting more than one type of data to answer your research question, or, in research terms, towards using a mixed method approach. This is not meant to be an inevitable decision, but we have a number of reasons that back up our stance. Firstly, we can see the positives and negatives of both qualitative and quantitative approaches. Both give valuable insight to answering a research question and therefore we tend to be loath to choose one in preference of the other. As teachers, we believe that it is important to know both what happened (quantitative evidence) as well as why it might have occurred (qualitative evidence).

Secondly, having worked in schools we accept the complexities of the classroom and the way in which it can impact on the research process. There is a need to be pragmatic in matching your research question with the evidence that is available and practical to collect. It is impossible to analyse all the variables which could impact on the outcome of a change or innovation and therefore more than one method aimed at answering a question can increase your confidence that you are matching cause and effect and answering your question. In this section, therefore, we want to exemplify how a multi-method approach can work, how different methods can work together to answer a research question and how collecting data from different perspectives can strengthen your 'case'.

At first, collecting more than one kind of data can seem to be a bit over the top, but when you keep in mind the broad definition of research evidence that was outlined in the previous section then this can become more manageable. So for example, in many of the projects where we have worked with teacher-researchers we have encouraged them to collect at least three different types of data. However, we emphasise that the majority of these data should be either collected anyway in school, or should fit in with teaching and learning or fit into existing school structures. In other words, out of three methods we are saying that at the most only one should be anything over and above what is done already. This can be seen in the diagram of an example research project below. The research question is answered using three different methods; however, two of them (method 1 and 3) are not going to impinge on normal practice. Only one of the data collection methods (method 2) is explicitly linked to the research process and therefore will need to be carefully added into the research plan due to time considerations.

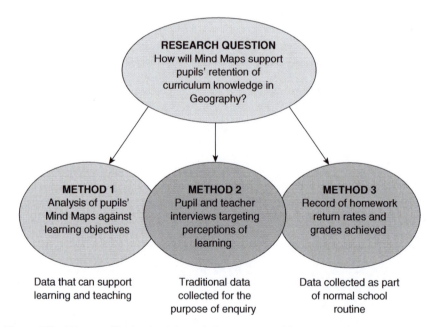

Figure 4.2   Diagram illustrating triangulation across evidence sources

So we would say that to make a multi-method approach practicable then you should mostly use evidence that you have to hand. However, it is useful also to think of the different types of evidence that you are collecting.

Returning to the idea that quantitative data is useful to show what happened, while qualitative data says why, both data types can be seen as useful for putting together the most comprehensive picture of the impact of an innovation or change. Therefore in thinking about the data collection techniques you use it is useful to think across the range of qualitative and quantitative sources. Again using the example above, the teacher has used two qualitative methods (methods 1 and 2) and one quantitative (method 3), and therefore will be able to say whether Mind Mapping impacted on homework returns and the marks achieved (exploring *what* the output of the innovation might have been) as well as the perspectives of the pupils and teachers and the Mind Map association with learning objectives (which will hopefully give some insight as to *why* the impact happened).

The final aspect to consider when confirming your choice of data collection should be the different perspectives, which might be impacted upon by the innovation which you have implemented and how these perspectives might be captured. In the table below, the perspectives of teaching staff and learners are focused on (although it might also be useful to think about parents and the wider school community). Here we are starting to think about the internal and external manifestation of the perspectives of these groups.

Table 4.3 Thinking about different perspectives on the same phenomenon

	INTERNAL	EXTERNAL
LEARNERS	Thinking Beliefs Attitudes	Behaviours Performance Examples of work
TEACHING STAFF	Thinking Beliefs Attitudes	Behaviours Performance Planning/marking

The external characteristics are more output based. In other words the perspectives of an individual can be observed or recorded. For example, a child who is finding a subject difficult might behave inappropriately in that lesson; or a teacher who is feeling underconfident with the new ICT equipment they have been given might avoid planning too many lessons using it. In both cases the external characteristics are reflecting the individual's perspective. The disadvantage of relying on this kind of data is that as a researcher you have to interpret the behaviours correctly and without the individual's input, you need to think about how confident you are that your third party interpretation is correct. This is where the internal perspectives become an important counterpoint. Individuals' and groups' beliefs and attitudes about an innovation are really important in exploring perspectives on an innovation. By asking what they believe then you are getting first hand what their perspective might be. However, it should be recognised that these first hand accounts can be tempered and impacted upon by how the individual reacts to your research agenda or you as a person. You need to consider power relationships (particularly when asking children what they think) and personal agendas that might prejudice the data.

There are, therefore, disadvantages and advantages to both these methods of capturing groups' perspectives, but again thinking about mixed methods and how you can combine different data collection methods can go some way to compensate and rationalise your research and what you want to get from it. Thinking carefully about the data that are already available, that which can be collected as part of teaching and learning or school routine, is useful in combining with more traditional methods; your research question is essential in making the process practical and, by using more than one method, increased confidence in the enquiry can be achieved.

There are many different ways of mixing methods. Creswell and Plano Clark (2007) give three main types of data mixing. These are outlined in the diagrams below. In the first type the two data collection tools contribute equally to the results (for example if you were looking at the impact of a pedagogic approach on attainment then you might collect course grades as well as teacher assessments). In the second there is a facilitatory relationship between the two data types with the first data collection tool informing the design and/or purpose of the second (for example, themes emerging from a series of interviews are used as the basis for the design of a questionnaire). The third shows a design where priority is given to one data type over another, but embedded in the design is a complementary source of data (for example, in a largely quantitative survey, a couple of open-ended questions might be included so that rich complementary data can be collected).

These models help you think about how the findings from the different data collection techniques come together to answer your enquiry question and what you are going to do if the answers conflict. Going back to the example enquiry above looking at Mind Maps in Geography, what would you do if the interviews find that the students and teachers really dislike the Mind Maps, while the grades and homework returns show a significant improvement? What would you 'make public' as your finding?

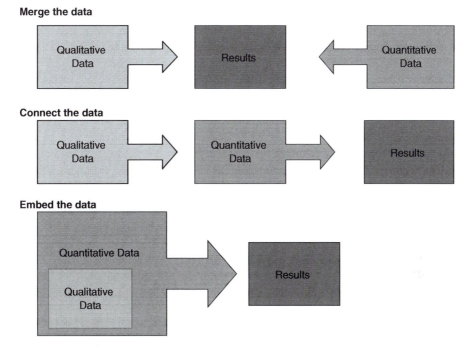

Figure 4.3   Different mixed methods models (adapted from Creswell and Plano Clark 2007)

This is where a strategic plan using Creswell and Plano Clark's three types is useful: be honest with yourself about which type of data is given precedence and the role that the different data sources will take in relation to each other.

Mixed methods are not just about the data collection stage. A commonly observed misconception is that researchers say they are undertaking mixed methods, but actually they are only collecting mixed data and when it comes to the synthesis, analysis and dissemination phases they revert to a single approach. So in addition to thinking about how the data collection tools will work together to answer your research questions you also need to think about how you can mix methods in later stages to increase the rigour of your enquiry. So for example, at analysis stage, outcomes from a questionnaire can be used as the basis for a thematic analysis of a series of interviews, or in another example, an analysis of work samples from a workshop could be used as the basis of an analysis of video. An example can be seen visually in the box below.

Ultimately, mixed method research is about trying to find the most convincing answer to your enquiry question as possible. By collecting both quantitative and qualitative data, by thinking about behaviours and attitudes, by using multiple data collection tools and by mixing analysis then

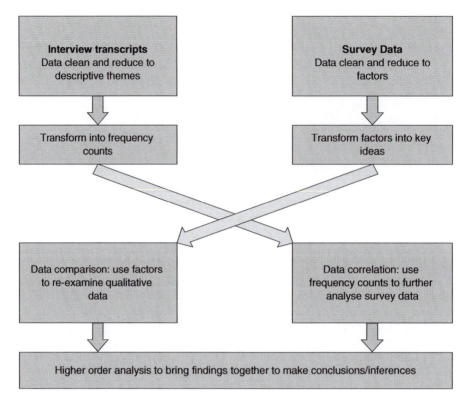

Figure 4.4   Example of mixed method analysis process

you are trying to increase the validity and reliability of your research. You must ensure that you remain strategic, with a sharp focus on answering your enquiry, but at the same time support a creative process that can explore different aspects of pedagogic practice.

Matching data collection tools to questions

In this chapter we have asked you to think about your research question and to make sure that it is answerable and manageable alongside your other teaching commitments. We have suggested that you think about different research approaches and weigh up the advantages and disadvantages of each with a target audience and potential sceptical colleague in mind. In addition, we have outlined the range of data that can be used in answering your research questions and the extent to which an overlap between your research and teaching and learning objectives in the classroom can be useful in balancing your own commitments as well as making the research as meaningful as possible.

The last thought we would like to leave you with as you head into the three chapters on collecting data from teachers, pupils, parents and the wider school community, is that whatever evidence you choose to use and whichever data collection tools you incorporate into your research design, you need to make sure that they link back and answer your research question. You need to make sure that the processes are manageable, that you can rationalise your choice of method and that you can achieve confidence that you have answered your question appropriately.

Key perspectives on research design

Bryman, A. (2008) *Social Research Methods* (3rd edn), Oxford: Oxford University Press.

Cohen, L., Manion, L. and Morrison, K. (2011) *Research Methods in Education* (7th edn). London: Routledge.

Denscombe, M. (2003) *The Good Research Guide* (2nd edn), Berkshire: Open University Press.

Lewis, I. and Munn, P. (1997) *So You Want to Do Research! A Guide for Beginners on How to Formulate Research Questions*. SCRE Publication No. 136. SCRE: Edinburgh.

References used in this chapter

Creswell, J.W. and Plano Clark, V.L. (2007) *Designing and Conducting Mixed Methods Research*. London: Sage Publications.

Prosser, J. (2007) 'Visual methods and the visual culture of schools', *Visual Studies*, 22(1), 13–30.

5

TAKING ACCOUNT OF LEARNER PERSPECTIVES IN YOUR ENQUIRY

Chapter enquiry questions

- How can you change the way you look at what is happening in your context?
- What might your learners have to tell you?
- Are there different ways to get at learners' experiences and ideas?
- How can you incorporate a range of voices in your enquiry?

Introduction

This chapter presumes that, as many practitioner enquirers do, you have made a decision to investigate learners in some way as part of your enquiry. This could be a consultation of attitudes or beliefs or it could be an exploration of learner behaviours or an investigation of learning outcomes. It could be with regard to institution structures, organisation and management or the process of teaching and learning. Regardless of the focus, this chapter will explore the different evidence sources that can be used to do this, the different methods that might be used and the issues and considerations that are important when researching learners' perspectives.

The UN Convention on the Rights of the Child (1989) gave momentum to the trend of asking children and young people their opinions on phenomena that impact on their lives. This has meant a steady increase in the prominence given to learners' voices in policy, practice and research (Ruddock, 2006). In the current context it is now accepted that learners be consulted about most aspects of their experience. Although the trend for asking learners opinions does increase with age, there are more studies exploring university students' perspectives than in early years' settings; children as young as three and four years old are now being consulted (for example, Clark et al., 2005). This means researchers are being increasingly innovative in the methodologies used to facilitate these conversations and therefore generate valid evidence (for example, Thompson, 2008; Greig and Taylor, 1999).

The Teaching and Learning Research Project (TLRP) (for example, James et al., 2007) dedicated a whole strand of research to this agenda and, led by the late Jean Ruddock and Donald McIntyre who pioneered so much of the innovation and debate in this area, produced many publications which drove the pupil voice agenda forwards (Arnot et al., 2004; Flutter and Ruddock, 2004). Yet the true potential of practices that draw on the process of pupil consultation often remains ambiguous due to a variety of constraints (Ruddock and McIntyre, 2007) and this appears to particularly be the case when the focus of the conversation moves away from the structures and organisation of school and towards the more contentious and arguably abstract focus of learning and teaching.

In practice, partly because of the inclusion of pupil voice in inspection criteria, but also through a genuine recognition of the stake that learners have in an education system, the consultation process is becoming increasingly participatory. However, it is not enough to ask for their opinion, but rather learners should be involved in the activity and have a stake in the process and outcomes. Hart's (1997) ladder of participation is useful in thinking about this move. When considering activities such as student councils/unions (Osler, 2000; Alderson, 2000) or 'students as researchers' initiatives (Raymond, 2001; Worrall, 2000) then we encourage you to consider the authenticity of the role the learners play and the warrant to take action that is given to them within the process as a result. After all, you will expect to learn from and make changes based on your enquiry process, so why shouldn't the learners expect the same? Too often learner voice activities are relatively meaningless and tokenistic with all the power remaining with the teachers and the school system.

Table 5.1   Plus/minus/interesting of pupil consultation

PLUS	MINUS	INTERESTING
New ways of looking	Time	Can pupil consultation techniques be incorporated into the curriculum?
Student investment	Lack of authenticity	
Impact on traditional roles/power dynamics		

It is useful to consider the different approaches to and perspectives on pupil consultation in your context. The table above might be helpful: what are the positives, what are the negatives and what are the things that make you think? There is little doubt that within the work we have done (as the quotes provided from teachers testify), investigation of the learners' perspective has been both informative and sometimes unexpectedly influential in informing institution development and innovation. It is not an unproblematic area of enquiry, but with careful thought and implementation you can reap the rewards.

There are many different factors driving initiatives that support learner voice, so it should be recognised that there are also differences associated with the way research is undertaken. This includes the contrast between quite formulaic consultation, which could be seen as ticking boxes on institution Self-Evaluation Forms (SEFs), and more formative processes, which can support institutional development as well as extending teachers' and learners' understanding of teaching and learning (Arnot et al., 2004). Given that there are so many different approaches to collecting data on learners, there is a real need to think through the reasons why you are asking learners for their perspective, what you think the outcomes will be and who the outcomes are for. One of our underlying theoretical ideas is that the enquiry cycle tends to lead the practitioner to a more formative and reflective process for themselves. The challenge when thinking about learner perspectives is to ask how findings relating to the learners are fed back to them as individuals; when and how they get a chance to validate (agree/disagree with) the interpretation of their views and when and how they get a say in the next step of the *action*. In our view this becomes an ethical issue, which needs to be considered before any consultation can be undertaken.

There is a big grey area around consultation and the concept of action that needs to be managed if learners are going to be consulted in a meaningful way. If students have the right to engage critically with learning and to be party to the teachers' underlying reasoning about the type of pedagogy and learning they are being involved in, then there also need to be common rules around the boundaries of those conversations and the limits in the actions that can be taken as a result. Teachers and students need to be able to critically engage with learning and its application to themselves and others; however real life situations mean that approaches may not best fit with all individuals' learning dispositions and styles at any one time and everyone needs to be happy to work around an outcome which has best fit with the group as a whole. In addition learners have to accept that teachers have undertaken training around teaching and learning and may know best (although arguably the reasoning behind this 'knowing best' should be transparent). An inclusive ethos about learning means that students and teachers have to have a pragmatic understanding of how learning is applied and received. Autonomy, transparency, adaptability and choice therefore become important in learner consultation: teachers can support children's engagement in different ways and children need to be able, within the constraints, to be creative in their engagement with these pedagogies.

This chapter will be based around the way in which learner views and perspectives can develop and accentuate feedback loops within the institution – the way in which research can be used to encourage communication about learning and teaching between different individuals in an institution, including the learners. The authors believe that underlying any true enquiry into the learners' perspective there must be an authenticity of process. In other words, there needs to be transparency and honesty in the way that the research is rationalised to the learners and also a commitment to involvement from the learners at more than a tokenistic level. In addition, it needs to be recognised that there is an outcome, an action, arising from the consultation for it to be meaningful and this also needs to be communicated across participants. Thus, by opening up the rationale to learners, the action research is not an isolated enquiry by an individual, but becomes an open dialogue about the processes operating in institutions and provides an evidence-based rationale for development and innovation.

We believe that there are three key research areas commonly examined with regard to the learners' perspective. These are:

- the observed behaviour (performative data);
- evidence of learning (data on cognitive outcomes as well as cognitive process); and
- learners' thinking and beliefs (data on attitude, dispositions and metacognition).

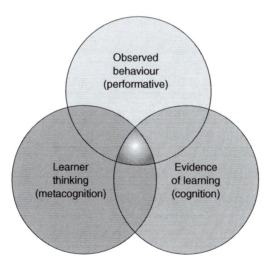

Figure 5.1   Key research areas for exploring the learners' perspective

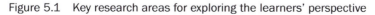

We see these different aspects as overlapping (see Figure 5.1); however, for ease of explanation they will be covered in turn within this chapter and for each section we will look at potential methods for enquiring into this aspects of the learners' perspective. However, it is always worth remembering the extent to which transfer and overlap can be made, particularly with regard to how one research method can explore more than one of these areas.

Within each section we will explore the extent to which evidence is already available, as previously stated institutions are data-rich environments, and learner-related data are no exception to this rule; we will ask to what extent can this be taken advantage of and whether this data collection can be extended in any way to make the process more formative and less 'box ticking' (as discussed above). We will also look at data that can be collected in a way that either takes advantage of institution structures that are already in place, for example, institution councils, or evidence that can support teaching and learning. We will also look at the third aspect, which is data that need to be collected in addition to the previous two, including how learners can operationalise their own enquiry and become researchers into their own learning.

Observable behaviours (performative data)

Performative data are the observable behaviours that learners (or indeed anyone else) exhibit in reaction to a change in normal practice. For example, a learner who does not appreciate a new approach to practical science might decide not to turn up to sessions (data that can be collected through attendance records); or they might express their opinion to the teacher or peers with regard to the changes (data which can be collected through the use of videoed lessons) or they may be observably more often off task in these lessons than in other lessons (data that can be collected through an on-task/off-task observation schedule). All of these look in some way at the outcome of the change as reflected in the learners' actions and behaviour: the external response.

To research learners' behaviour, data collected from students routinely as part of the day to day running of an institution and the normal process of teaching and learning seems to be a fairly reasonable option. For example, in most educational establishments work and attainment are routinely assessed, attendance is monitored and behaviours observed (from informal classroom management to formal behaviour monitoring). These processes and the resulting data can easily be used as part of an enquiry; indeed we would positively encourage their use as a source of evidence as they help to make the research practicable, meaningful and relevant. This could be done either by looking across data sources but focusing on one or two children as individual case studies using a tracking document like the one in Table 5.1; or it could be done using one or two data sources, but focusing across classes, year groups or institutions to give the wider trends. As the data is already collected, it is just a matter of synthesising it, analysing it and reporting it in such a way that it answers your enquiry question, rather than doing anything new or different.

Having said this there are various ways in which this cross-over between teaching and research can be made more explicit and therefore more manageable. Learner tracking is a useful way of collecting and triangulating data that is routinely collected in institutions, giving an overview of specific learners' institution experience. Table 5.2 gives a range of different data types that might be collected and encourages you to think about the timescale around which you might structure this collection. This list is in no way exhaustive and the timings will vary between institutions, but as a broad outline it has been shown to be useful. The enquirer needs to be critical in thinking about what is available in their context and what answers their research question.

It might be that existing data in your institution are not enough or suitable to answer your enquiry question. If this is the case then you will need to think about another way of investigating learner behaviours. This is likely to be some form of observation schedule in its most traditional sense. This research method may need a third person, or some training for learners if they are to use it, but can provide very specific and consistent information about the behaviours of learners at different points in a lesson or as a comparison across sessions. A popular observation schedule, which has been used across projects and age groups, is the 'on-task/off-task behaviour observation' (see in Figure 5.2).

Table 5.2 Example of pupil tracking data

Data	Timescale					
	Year	Semester	Term	Month	Week	Day
Standardised test scores						
National Student Survey						
Teacher assessments						
Individual education plans						
Work samples						
Behaviour logs						
VLE log-in rates						
Parental consultation records						
Homework return rates						
Attendance						

SYSTEMATIC OBSERVATION OF INDIVIDUAL PUPILS								
SCHOOL:	Observe the pupil every 5 minutes and record their behaviour at the time		BEHAVIOURS	Tally Chart of Observed Behaviours for 5 Focus Pupils				
				Pupil 1	Pupil 2	Pupil 3	Pupil 4	Pupil 5	Total
CLASS:		ON TASK	Talk related to task					
DATE:			Answering question					
			At work					
LESSON:			Listening to teacher/peer					
TEACHER:		OFF TASK	Talk not task related					
SUBJECT:			Wandering around room					
			Attempting to draw attention					
OBSERVATION:			Day dreaming					
			Total					

Figure 5.2   On-task/off-task observation sheet

This observation schedule is based on a process of time-sampling. It is very difficult for an observer to keep accurate and consistent observations continually for more than 10 minutes and so this is why time-sampling is essential. Time-sampling means that observations are taken for just a percentage of the lesson or environment being observed. The main ways this can be done is through:

- Chunking; or
- Scanning.

Chunking refers to a focused observation of specific learner or group of learners over a 'chunk' of time, typically ten minutes or more. This kind of close tracking allows you to understand how learners manage their learning, how they interact with others and how they move from one state to another. It is hard to do this kind of observation whilst simultaneously teaching, so normally a third party – perhaps a colleague – might perform the observation or video would be used. Scanning means that the whole area is scanned every two, five or ten minutes (the timing is chosen depending on manageability and context) and the behaviours observed at each moment in time are noted down through a tally. A picture is built up over time. This observation schedule allows you to focus on a specific group of learners (chosen as either representative of the class or because their characteristics fit with the nature of the enquiry) and identify their predominant behaviours over the duration of the lesson. The example below comes from a primary school where on-task/off-task observations were completed by a member of teaching staff with the aim of exploring Year 1 children's behaviours in different learning environments over an academic year.

Primary School Example

Observation of the class indicated that children had become more motivated in their own learning. Over the year they appeared to become less reliant on the teacher to direct their learning and keep them focused and on task. The children began to appear excited when making their choice of activity and looked forward to visiting the different learning environments.

	Number of pupils and total time spent on task				
	0–9 mins	10–19 mins	20–29 mins	30–39 mins	40–45 mins
Autumn 2nd	4	2	4	5	0
Spring 1st	2	2	6	4	1
Spring 2nd	0	3	2	6	4
Summer 1st	0	0	4	3	8
Summer 2nd	0	0	0	0	15

When carrying out formal observations on five separate occasions over the year it was evident that the number of children who remained on task (motivated to learn) for the duration of the self-initiated session (L2L session) had dramatically risen.

(Continued)

(Continued)

During the summer term observation, out of the fifteen children observed in the session, all remained on task for 40–45 minutes (the duration of the session), an improvement on the other half terms and a considerable improvement on the autumn 2nd and spring 1st half term.

The same group of children were observed on each separate occasion and it is evident from the findings that there was a 100 per cent increase on the number of learners who remained on task for the duration of the lesson in the summer compared to the autumn. It is, however, not possible to conclude if the increased age and maturity of the learners over the year could have contributed to the findings and, if so, how much.

These observed behaviours can stand alone as research evidence to support teaching and learning, but you need to consider whether this is truly the learners' perspective or whether it is learner outcomes only and how this might reflect different answers to your research question. Both have their value, but to increase the meaningfulness of your enquiry it is often better to also ask the learners about the context surrounding these behaviours and why they might have happened (either a questionnaire or an interview). It is important to ask whether it is right to always assume that a learner who is repeatedly observed off-task in your lessons does not like your new thinking skills pedagogy or whether there is something more complicated going on. To check your assumptions or to explore this complexity further then the evidence could be used more directly as the starting point for an interview with a specific learner or the whole class. In this way the evidence, attendance, homework return rates, etc., are presented to the learners and they are asked to explain what they think the results mean and rationalise any oddities in the data or consider how it could be changed. Through using either of these approaches the whole direction of the consultation and involvement of learners in the enquiry changes. If we return to the three-way Venn diagram introduced previously, then this is where you start to cross over from performative data to learners' thinking: you are not only recording and analysing the observable behaviours, but also exploring the learner's reasoning as to why they happened.

Before moving on to learner thinking however, it is useful to spend a small amount of time focusing on one more approach to collecting performative data: video. Video is a useful tool for gathering data that can be returned to repeatedly, allowing in-depth analysis of behaviour. Indeed by setting it up to record in the room where you are teaching, then you can also capture the relationship between your own and learners' behaviours, which can provide further insight. Some tips as to the practicalities of using video in the classroom are included in Figure 5.3 below and these issues should not be underestimated.

Top tips for using video in a learning environment

- Make sure that there is sufficient tape or space on a disc (if digital video)
- Work out where the electricity points are in the classroom (your cable may not be long enough)
- If using a battery, make sure that there is enough power for the recording you want to do
- Try not to swoop and zoom too much, too quickly as it's difficult to watch later
- Try to avoid zooming in on learners as it can cause a distraction
- Do an on-the-spot trial and replay to make sure you are recording
- Make sure that your sound equipment is adequate. It is often difficult to discern individual voices in a classroom environment and this can make the process of transcription even more demanding
- Think about the purpose of your study and the operation of the camera. If you want to observe whole class interaction in order to develop an hypothesis about your teaching behaviour, for example, then you will have to think about camera position and how you will introduce it.
- **Make sure** that you have received **parental** and **learner permission** prior to recording. This is essential given the possibility of religious objections and current policies on child protection issues. Check the institution and local council policies prior to sending out a letter requesting permission
- Make sure all parties concerned agree to later access rights (to the recordings) as this will impact on parental consent (especially for children on an 'at risk' register). This is particularly important if you are thinking of putting any visual images in a publication or on an internet site. The NSPCC website provides useful recommendations:

  http://www.nspcc.org.uk/Inform/trainingandconsultancy/consultancy/helpandadvice/helpandadvice_wda47843.html

---

Figure 5.3   Tips for using video

Using video is a really effective way of collecting comprehensive data from a context, plus it has the advantage of replay so that you can revisit the data as your enquiry develops. On the down side, it can create a vast amount of data to be analysed (sometimes an overwhelming amount, particularly for a busy teacher). However, there are ways in which it can be made manageable. This could be through limiting the amount of time that is to be included as footage for the research or by limiting analysis specifically to the question that you want to answer. For example, focus on a specific section of a lesson like plenaries, targeting a specific group working together rather than the whole class for the whole of the lesson automatically concentrates the data for your enquiry (an example of this approach can be seen in the case study from Hebden Green Special School below); or if the whole lesson is necessary, steer the analysis of the footage by being clear about what you are looking for and limiting the way in which it is used. This could be done by focusing on just the questions asked by the teachers and how they are responded to; by targeting your analysis to the behaviours of a specific sample of children (who can be chosen for a variety of reasons: a representative sample, individual characteristics etc.); or by using a coding scheme which targets the evidence you need to answer your research question.

Developing Question & Answer Sessions for Pupils with Communication Difficulties

Stacey Cartner and Katy Richards

Hebden Green Special School, Cheshire West and Chester

OBJECTIVES

We focused specifically on 'learning relationships and interaction in the classroom', as so much of what we do is based on a strong and effective relationship between staff and learners and learners and their peers that we really felt that this was the area to focus on. 'Tools for learning' is the other area we focused on as if we can provide the children with these tools, then they have them for life to use whenever necessary, to continue their learning journey throughout their life.

HYPOTHESIS

Does developing personalised learning in question and answer sessions for pupils with various communication difficulties, focusing on the use of application and analysis based questions, improve engagement and speaking and listening skills?

RESEARCH PROCESS

To record our data we chose to video a question/answer session in two classes, one in the primary and one in the secondary section of the school. We chose this method because of the range of abilities and communication strategies within each group; other methods could not record the subtleties of communication within the classroom.

Although this method provided us with a huge range of data it also meant that to have a piece of text that could be analysed we had to go through the lengthy process of transcribing chosen parts of our video. It still did not record strategies such as eye contact and facial expression.

We each recorded one session prior to implementing the intervention and one towards the end of the academic year. We decided to do this because they clearly show the progress made by the learners during this time and the progress of our own teaching strategies.

FINDINGS

In the initial video (Autumn Term 2007) for both Y8 and Y2, knowledge and comprehension questions were used most frequently. We were already aware that this may be the result shown in the video and accompanying tally chart and transcript.

In the second video for both groups there was a clear progression in the types of questions used. This was achieved in two different ways to make the lessons age appropriate. In Y2 the teacher changed her approach to ensure that she was including a wider range of questions and giving the children more opportunity to develop their learning and understanding in a practical situation. In Y8 the teacher facilitated the learning by giving pupils the opportunity to develop their own questioning skills.

There was clearly a difference between the two groups studied; this could be for a number of reasons:

- Developmentally, the Y8 group had progressed to initiating their own communication and had less reliance on the teacher;
- Pupils in the Y8 group had more independent speech and less reliance on signing and symbol boards, although communication difficulties were still present;
- Interaction in the Y2 group was still dominated by the teacher in video 2, although the range of interactions and questions was greater.

As before with the learner tracking data, research with video can be made into a more formative process of enquiry by involving the learners in the process of video capture as well as the analysis. With the former, where learners have been given the job of taking the video with a specific focus in mind, then an additional level of data analysis can be based upon what the learners chose to film and their rationale for it:

- Why did you film this?
- Why did you not film that?
- Why do you think it is a good example of the teaching and learning you're interested in?

The quote below comes from a case study written by a teacher in a nursery institution (learners in the target class ranged in age from three to four and eight months) and shows how video cameras were used to support the learners in enquiring into their own and their peers' learning, while also supporting the enquiry of the teacher at a meta-level. The footage was not only useful for the children in thinking about what learning looked like; it helped the teachers' understanding and when shown to parents, highlighted to them the way in which learning can be facilitated in the nursery setting.

Infant School Example

The children were fascinated by the video camera so Mrs H introduced a small hand-held camera for the children to use. This was very exciting for them and they all wanted to try. Obviously, it was not as easy as it looked and the less able children struggled. However, she persevered and a number of children were able to record their friends' activities.

Some children even had the confidence to ask questions as they were recording their friends' activities. The whole group enjoyed watching the 'play-back' and it encouraged more children to have a try.

As the children became accustomed to the presence of the camera, they soon forgot about it and some excellent work was recorded. One section of the film which was very useful to show parents was a child 'reading' a 'Percy' book to her friend during milk time. She was able to follow conventions such as giving the title of the book, turning the pages carefully and showing the illustrations. She also repeated the story almost word perfect and showed obvious enjoyment while doing so.

Involving the learners in the analysis of video can also be useful, particularly to initiate a discussion about learning. Specific sections can be used as prompts or for an interview (for example, *what you were doing here was interesting; can you talk me through what was going on?*) or the learners can be asked to choose specific bits and talk about what is happening and why (for example, *I am interested in effective group work; can you choose for me a video clip which you feel represents this and tell me why you chose it?*). In this way the learners themselves are interpreting the videoed behaviours. This increases the meaningfulness of the interpretation and therefore the validity of the research is increased.

Evidence of learning (cognition)

Evidence of learning is the main 'business' of education institutions. Using our broader understanding of evidence, introduced in Chapter 4, means many different data sources emerge from this activity. If we focus on assessment, then this can include standardised attainment data (for example, GCSE results), teacher assessments, peer assessment and self-assessment of learning. Each has its advantages and disadvantages, often related to the summative or formative nature of different assessment types, and as a researcher you need to approach each from a critical standpoint and make sure that the most appropriate is chosen for answering your research question and for triangulating with other data collected. However teaching and learning are not just about assessment; they are also about the process of cognition (the thinking process), which is arguably harder to capture, but can be explored through observations of talk in the classroom (this could be, for example, learner–learner or teacher–learner talk).

Standardised assessments are commonly used in education research projects. This is because it is a language that policy makers appear to recognise and pay attention to. It is a common perception that for an innovation to be effective then it needs to raise standards, standards as measured by recognised national tests. This is also a popular and commonly understood discourse in institutions and associated communities. It is a language (of subjects, curriculum and grades/levels) that is easily recognised and is one that tends to dominate much of the management level conversation about teaching and learning. As such this type of data is useful to collect as part of your research and, if there is an improvement in results, can have a tendency to convince more people of an innovation's success. However, finding a direct relationship between a raised score in standardised tests and a single innovation is difficult. There is so much going on in any one institution, so many new innovations. Change and development related to institution structures, to curriculum and to pedagogy are endemic at the moment, and so pinpointing which may have actually caused the change with complete confidence is hard and often unrealistic. That doesn't mean that it is not useful to try.

In the example below a secondary teacher has completed an action research project using GCSE results to explore the impact of a peer-mentoring process.

In this box it is possible to see that the teacher has compared the GCSE results for two groups in the same Year 11: those involved in the mentoring programme and those that were not.

Secondary School Example

Twenty five students took part in the mentoring programme. These were students whose performance in their GCSE exams was giving cause for concern. They were statistically capable of grade C in a number of subjects (five or more) but were, according to teacher assessment data, working below or well below this level in most subjects.

Fifteen of the 25 students gained 5 A*–C grades, a success rate of 60%. Of the 240 separate GCSE examinations taken by this cohort, the results in the top three grades were:

- 3 A grades
- 27 B grades
- 86 C grades

48% of the grades gained by this cohort were A*–C. It should also be noted that had four of the students managed to turn one of their D grades into a C, the success rate for the cohort would have been 76%. The graph summarises the results for 44 students targeted. It can be seen that 60% of students in the target group who engaged in the programme gained 5 A*–C grades, whereas, 30% of students in the target group who did not engage in the programme gained 5 A*–C grades.

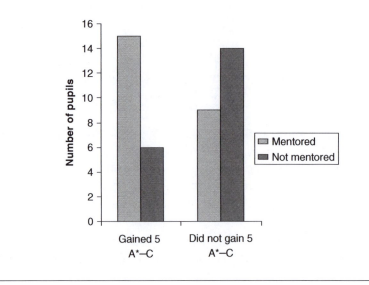

The results achieved in this action research project are fairly convincing, but the extent to which a direct correlation can be assumed between the mentoring project and the GCSE results has to be considered: for example,

- Were the groups comparable before the intervention?
- What else was going on in the school?
- What teacher effects might have influenced the data?

This is not to dismiss the finding, but just to put into context and consider the variables that could also have impacted on the cohorts. Researching in real life means that there will always be complicating factors.

There are also ethical issues tied up in using experimental/control research designs like this: as a teacher, you have to ask whether it is ethical to implement an innovation which you believe in to one group of learners and not another. These learners will not have the chance to do their GCSEs again and so are you disadvantaging one group for the benefit of the research process? If on the other hand the whole year group is included in an innovation, results would need to be compared in an alternative way, for example by comparing with mean data across previous year groups (a mean should account for any year group variation) or by relying on comparing predicted with actual data. As before, each has potential consequences, advantages and disadvantages relating to the research and pedagogic process, and so decisions have to be carefully made and rationalised.

In addition, as teachers we tend to have certain suspicions about the accuracy of the picture a test can provide of an individual's ability in a subject. An exam is arguably only testing certain types of cognitive ability, knowledge-based understanding, rather than skills and dispositions. Therefore your enquiry exams only show one type of cognitive outcome. This argument is slightly simplified, but for a pedagogic innovation to work it has to ideally do more than raise test results; it also needs to improve specific skills, vocabulary, motivation, aspirations and attitudes. One way in which, as a practitioner enquirer, you can feel more confident with your results as being a true reflection of the learning associated with your chosen innovation is to use other sources of information and triangulate them (as spoken about in Chapter 4). In other words, come at the evidence of learning from two (or even three) different directions. So this could be a triangulation of national tests with teacher assessments. Or it could be that results are backed up by the learners' opinion, gathered through interviews or questionnaires, about their own learning and their experience of the test themselves. In this way national tests are incorporated into the overall research design, but do not become overly relied upon.

So you need to think about the cognitive outcomes you expect if your intervention works and think about the data that can be gathered in addition to test scores. The popularity of formative assessment strategies (based on the work of Black and Wiliam (1998) and Clark et al. (2001) in institutions, for example, currently means that there is a developing dimension of peer assessment and self-assessment which can be easily incorporated into action research, while also relating closely to dialogue about teaching and learning in the classroom.

There are many outputs to formative assessment strategies that can become data collection tools. For example this could include:

- email conversations;
- contributions to online discussion forums;
- learning logs;
- peer-assessment records;
- records of the learners' use of three stars and a wish; or
- records of self-assessment activities (in the picture below this has been done using feeling fans, but many other approaches could be used).

All these activities are likely to be part of a teacher's pedagogy, while also, without too much additional effort, become a collection of data to support an enquiry.

The data collection strategies above all rely on some kind of recordable outcome, but this is difficult when thinking about cognitive *process* data. Yet this is an additional element to thinking about cognition: it is not just the test score, but how a student achieved it that is of interest. So we need to

Figure 5.4   Photograph of children using feeling fans to indicate their understanding in a lesson

think about whether there is a way of gathering evidence of learning in action. Group work, discussion and dialogue about learning are all important pedagogical strategies and so it is important that evidence of learning does not just become dominated by assessment, whether formative or summative. This type of learning can be evidenced through the incorporation of some kind of output into a task, for example:

- take photographs (which could be annotated by the learners) of the different stages of a practical activity (see example below);
- allocate role of scribe within each group with job of recording discussion;
- tape or video record discussions in class;
- get learners to record main points of discussion; or
- create before and after topic mind maps of subject knowledge.

Primary School Example

The teacher wanted the whole class to be involved in the process and so had to design a strategy which was appropriate and achievable for all 22 children, while also being manageable. The children were very confident in saving, retrieving and creating files in many applications and they were also comfortable with downloading pictures and placing them in documents. Even though they had not been taught how to use *PowerPoint* or how to create and add sound files, they acquired these skills very quickly and easily.

In groups of three or four the children were asked to design an ancient Greek monster with at least one part to move using pneumatics. They had an afternoon to design, create and evaluate the monsters and after every half an hour a digital photograph of the model was taken and the children were asked to write down where they were in the design process and any adaptations they had been forced to make.

This list is in no way exhaustive; there are all sorts of ways in which this kind of task can be tweaked to provide evidence. Think of practical elements to your teaching and learning (for example, experimental science, fieldwork, performance or group work) and how you can record the learning that is taking place; think about how you do it as a teacher and then how you can incorporate this into your enquiry. This is the kind of evidence that can be incorporated into the teaching and learning process (see Chapter 4).

Learner thinking and beliefs

Learners' thinking behind observed behaviour and behind evidence of learning is the third section we want to explore in this chapter. In comparison to previously described data, this section could be criticised as being 'soft' data: data that rely on the learners' honest appraisal and explanation of 'what is going on in their heads'. That is not to say these data are any less important than other types; indeed, we would argue that they provide an invaluable complementary data source which add depth to any enquiry. As you will probably have noticed throughout this chapter it has regularly been proposed that learners should be consulted on data to be part of the process of curiosity and explanation. For example, on-task/off-task observation data, video footage, self-assessment and national test scores can all stand alone, but if used as a starting point for dialogue with learners then the reasons behind a particular outcome might start to become clear.

Talk is fundamental to all teaching contexts and therefore to open up a dialogue about an aspect of teaching and learning as part of an enquiry might appear to be a logical step. There are many different ways in which a learner can be consulted through the medium of talk, but arising from traditional qualitative research methodology, interviewing tends to be the most commonly thought of and recognised. It is also a method that many teachers feel comfortable with. However, it has to be asked at what point does a discussion about learning, for example, become data collection and at what point is it a pedagogical strategy? Can the purposes of each overlap? How does this impact on your research intent?

Interviews in their purest form consist of a set of questions to be answered verbally either on a one to one basis or as part of a group. An example of an interview schedule used to explore student researchers' experiences can be seen below. At a certain level it does not matter whether you are interviewing children or adults; there are certain things that need to be considered as part of any research. These include the level of structure provided in the interview schedule, the method for recording the communication and the way in which the data are to be analysed. However with children, particularly younger ones, there are a number of additional issues to be considered with regard to this method. For example, it is sometimes perceived that the tighter the structure, the better, thus leaving less scope for the topic of conversation to go off at a tangent. However, it does depend on the aim of the research. There might be occasions where an unstructured, immediate response is more useful than something that has been prompted for and thoroughly signposted. For example, we have seen successful enquiries where the Teacher-researcher has gone into the playground with one key question and asked a random sample of learners for their immediate response, whereas we have also seen structured interviews being used consistently across a class.

As a general rule, we would suggest that some kind of predetermined structure is helpful, although it does not have to be characterised through the traditional semi-structured interview schedule – a task or activity can mediate the interview just as successfully. We have had lots of success using visual mediation (see the section in Chapter 4): a sorting activity or a group mind-mapping activity can provide enough structure to focus learner responses effectively without the interviewer dominating too much.

Interview Schedule

Students as researchers

The aim of this interview is to reflect on and explore what it has been like to be involved as a student researcher at your institution. We are interested in what you did over the term and a half you have been involved, what changes you think the process has produced and how it affects your feelings about research and the institution. We're also interested in how the research has happened: the factors that enabled it and also any barriers that might have acted against it.

1　**Describe the process of your research over the last term and a half.**

    a　Why do you think the SMT asked you?
    b　Before the project started what were you most excited about?
    c　Before the project started what were your main worries about the project?
    d　How has the research process developed over the project?
    e　What would you do differently if you were to do the research again?
    f　What do you think should be the next step for the student as researcher group?

2　**What do you feel have been the main outputs of the research?**

    a　For you?
    b　For the group of student researchers?
    c　For the institution?
    d　Do you think you have learnt anything new?
    e　What skills have you acquired, if any?
    f　Do you think you will use the research skills again? If so, when?

3　**You have given presentations on your findings to the SMT, the staff and parents. What did that feel like?**

    a　Did you feel like your findings were taken seriously?
    b　Do you think there were any differences between these audiences?

(Continued)

Figure 5.5   *(Continued)*

   c What were the main worries about doing something like this?

   d What were you most excited about?

4 What would you say to a teacher who was thinking about initiating a similar student research group?

   a What do you think are the advantages of using student researchers?

   b What do you think are the disadvantages of using student researchers?

   c What would you advise other students about doing this type of research?

   d What would you advise another institution that wanted to use student researchers?

Figure 5.5   Example of a semi-structured interview schedule

When interviewing children, as an adult, you need to be aware of the impact you can have on the discourse. Teaching is probably the one profession where we routinely ask questions we know the answer to and therefore children become highly accomplished at 'guessing what the teacher is thinking'. There are also well established understandings of power that exist in education institutions that can impact on the data being collected (Robinson and Taylor, 2007), especially as represented by the learner–teacher relationship. Some of these characteristics are impossible to get away from and therefore within your enquiry you need to recognise their existence and then move on, but there are strategies you can employ to try and lessen the impact. One such strategy might be allocating to other learners the role of interviewer (many of the strategies talked about in this section can be applied to learner interviewers) or the use of a mediated interview. This is what happened in the case study below. Here it was the headteacher who was also the enquirer and she was very aware of the impact her role could have on the responses given by her first school pupils (age 4 to 9 years old).

Using Marking Ladders to Support Children's Self-Assessment in Writing

Victoria Symons and Deborah Currans

Wooler First School, Northumberland

RESEARCH QUESTION

How effective are marking ladders in supporting children's self-assessment of their own writing?

PROCESS

Prior to starting the project we spent some time as a staff discussing and simplifying the Lancashire Grid for Learning marking ladders, focusing on changing the language to make them more child friendly. We decided to focus more on children assessing what they had done in their writing rather than at this stage expecting them to know what to do next; it was about encouraging independence.

Therefore we customised the original LGfL marking ladders to make the tool more suited to the needs of our children. Eventually this came to a point where we involved the children in the design and creation of their own marking ladder. The process we went through is described in the following diary extracts.

RESEARCH PROCESS

A variety of research tools were used including pupil views templates, teacher–pupil interviews, work samples and examples of marking ladders.

In addition the children interviewed each other twice; this was felt to be better than one of the teachers doing the interviewing because of the power dynamics involved. We wanted honesty and this was felt best achieved through this approach. Indeed the children learned a lot by being the interviewer and this ultimately helped their thinking about learning.

The interviewee chose a piece of work in October and July to talk about and then the interviewer asked questions about their choice and how marking

(Continued)

91

(Continued)

ladders had helped. This was videoed and analysed at a later date. This process captured children's opinions about the marking ladders and any changes in their views about their learning.

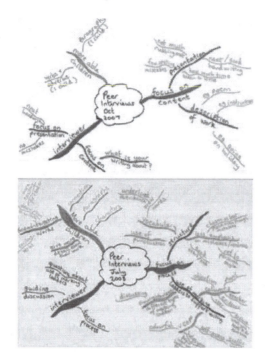

FINDINGS

We found that marking ladders were a useful tool to support children's self-assessment of their own writing and help them to focus on the process of writing. However it is important that marking ladders remain adaptable and can be differentiated for different abilities, especially for the more able. Overall they are effective but have to be adapted to suit the pupils and the context.

The mediated interview is one that is structured or supported by an object or process. With children, particularly young ones, an interview can be more successful if the talk is additional to another task with which they feel familiar, for example a work sheet, an object used as a discussion point or sorting activity (tasks that keep the child in the *comfort zone* of institution, but can also be targeted towards the outcome of the enquiry). Theoretically, through mediating an interview such potential influences as power relationships between learner and teacher, and 'guess what the teacher wants to know' scenarios, can be somewhat avoided.

With pupil views templates (Wall and Higgins, 2006) the template is designed as a 'semiotic tool' (Vygotsky, 1978) and forms the basis of the interview about the teaching activity. By providing an image of the learning situation on which the research is focusing, such as working in a group, or using a computer, the process becomes a three-way interaction between the Teacher-researcher, the learners and the template. The Teacher-researcher has an important role within the process of the interview; they initiate the discussion around the chosen learning context and to a certain extent will steer the dialogue. The cartoon image operates as a reminder of the specific learning context under discussion and thus acts as a stimulus; however, as part of the technique it is annotated by the child and therefore becomes a record of the discussion and a stimulus for further talk and elaboration.

Ideas from the discussion are recorded on the template. Throughout the interview learners are reminded and encouraged to write down their thoughts and ideas in the appropriate bubble. However, we usually emphasise that they need not worry about writing conventions (for example, spelling or grammar) but should complete the template in their own way: some learners have independently used one speech bubble for positive and one for negative impacts on learning; others added their own bubbles for extra space; and a few used drawings to illustrate their meaning. An example of a how a template was used can be seen in the example from Fleecefield Primary School, Enfield.

The Possibilities for Paired Learning in the Primary Institution

Emma Glasner and Ulfët Mahmout

Fleecefield Primary School, Enfield

HYPOTHESIS

We believe that, gender, ability and friendship focused paired work will create a more articulate, emotionally safer environment and improve children's academic performance.

(Continued)

(Continued)

RESEARCH PROCESS

To complement the observations we used a 'Pupil Views Template' (see below). We chose one which would enable the children to express the kind of talk they had experienced in the morning's lessons. It was presented to the children in the same way in both classes using the same language, asking the children to reflect on lessons in the morning covering the same content.

RESULTS

In the control class none of the children related the responses of the children in the pictures to the lesson on 'Goodnight Mr Tom'. In fact, one child imagined it had been a Spanish lesson. For example:

> *Hmm, what's that number on Amelia's worksheet. I'll never pass if I do it myself.*

It appears they were predominantly concerned with passing tests and many of the thoughts they ascribed to the template were about rewards or unrelated activities like football and discos. An example of this association between grades and rewards can be seen in the template completed by a child in the control class (included below).

Within the control class, there was little or no interaction between the two children shown in the picture and where thoughts were related to the other child, they seemed in competition with each other.

In the paired learning class all the templates reflected the lesson that they had participated in that morning. The characters in it were always conversing with each other and working together. They made explicit references to how they were working things out and who was responsible for the various roles within their partnership (see below).

They also ascribed value to their partner in their thoughts and some mentioned how it enabled them to achieve or enjoy the work:

Do you need help? OK let's work together.

What this all shows us is not that, if asked specifically, Indigo children, in the control class, could not talk about their learning, and/or never learn from their peers. But rather that paired learning in Lilac Class, the experimental group, had created an environment where that kind of talk and knowledge about how you work, your strengths and weaknesses is required. Thus it becomes something you draw upon without being pressed for it.

SUMMARY

In summary we have found that children's positive attitudes to working with each other are invaluable and we suspect that it has influenced them in the playground as well, as they are a very cohesive group this year in Lilac Class, which was not the case in Year 5. We are also amazed at how on-task the talk and support has made them.

Developing feedback loops

Researching the learners' perspective of learning and teaching can be a rewarding and insightful aspect of any enquiry. As 'learner voice' becomes more prevalent in institutions, teachers are finding that all learners, regardless of age, can have useful things to say about their experiences of the institution, teaching and learning. However, we would argue that there is a need to make sure that the process is truly authentic and to do this the process needs to be as transparent as possible.

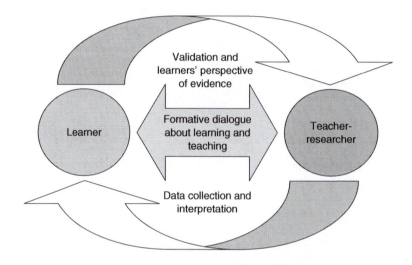

Figure 5.6   Diagram of how pupil consultation can support formative feedback loops

Throughout this chapter we have emphasised the need to open up the evidence to the learners, and even where it has been collected without their full participation, there is a rationale for getting their perspective on the outcome. In other words, by asking the learners about the data that has been collected about them, for example, attendance figures, behaviour observations and work samples, you then add a further dimension to your enquiry and validate the interpretations that you are making. Ultimately, this means opening up the research process to a sustained dialogue about learning and teaching and it is important that this dialogue includes not only other adults, but also learners. In this way not only will your enquiry be fuelled by different perspectives, but also the evidence can support a developmental process of thinking and building understanding about learning. This type of feedback loop will then benefit not only your own practice, but also the learners' thinking about their own learning and development.

Key perspectives on the learner's point of view

This is a growing area of interest for teachers, policy makers and academics, with some debate about the role of learners in the process and how far their views inform practice decisions.

Arnot, M., McIntyre, D., Pedder, D. and Reay, D. (2004) *Consultation in the Classroom: Developing Dialogue about Teaching and Learning.* Cambridge: Pearson Publishing.

Clark, J., Dyson, A., Meagher, N., Robson, E. and Wootten, M. (2001) 'Involving Young People in Research: The Issues'; In *Young People As Researchers: Possibilities, Problems, and Politics.* York: Youth Work Press.

Fielding, M. (2001) 'Beyond the rhetoric of student voice: new departures or new constraints in the transformation of 21st century institutioning?', *FORUM*, 43 (2): 100–110.

Flutter, J. and Ruddock, J. (2004) *Consulting Learners: What's in it for institutions?* London: Routledge Falmer.

Wall, K., Higgins, S. and Packard, E. (2007) *Talking about Learning: Using Templates to Find Out about Learner Views.* Plympton: Southgate Publishers.

References used in this chapter

Alderson, P. (2000) 'Institution students' views on institution councils and daily life at institution', *Children and Society*, 14(2): 121.

Arnot, M., McIntyre, D., Pedder, D. and Reay, D. (2004) *Consultation in the Classroom.* Cambridge: Pearson Publishing.

Black, P. J., & Wiliam, D. (1998) 'Inside the black box: Raising standards through classroom assessment'. *Phi Delta Kappan*, 80(2), 139–148.

Clark, J., Dyson, A., Meagher, N., Robson, E. and Wootten, M. (2001) 'Involving Young People in research: The Issues'. In Clark, J., Dyson, A., Meagher, N., Robson, E., Wootten, M., ed. *Young People As Researchers: Possibilities, Problems, and Politics.* York: Youth Work Press, 2001, pp. 1–10.

Clark, A., Kjorholt, A.T. and Moss, P. (2005) *Beyond Listening: Children's Perspectives on Early Childhood Services*, Bristol: Policy Press.

Flutter, J. and Ruddock, J. (2004) *Consulting Learners: What's in it for institutions?* London: Routledge Falmer.

Flutter, J. and Rudduck, J. (2004) *Consulting Pupils: What's in it for schools?* London: Routeldge Falmer.

Greig, A. & Taylor, J. (1999) *Doing Research with Children.* Thousand Oaks, CA: Sage.

Hart, R. (1997) *Children's Participation in Sustainable Development.* Abingdon: Earthscan.

James, M., McCormick, R., Black, P., Carmichael, P., Drummond, M-J., Fox, A., MacBeath, J., Marshall, B., Pedder, D., Procter, R., Swaffield, S., Swann, J. and Wiliam, D. (2007) *Improving Learning How to Learn: Classrooms, Schools and Networks.* London: Routledge.

Osler, A. (2000) 'Children's Rights, Responsibilities and Understandings of Institution Discipline', *Research Papers in Education*, 15(1): 49–67.

Raymond, L. (2001) 'Student Involvement in Institution Improvement: from data source to significant voice', *FORUM*, 43(2): 58–61.

Robinson, C. and Taylor, C. (2007) 'Theorizing Student Participation: values and perspectives', *Improving Schools*, 10(5): 5–17.

Ruddock, J. (2006) 'The Past, The Papers and The Project' (Editorial), *Educational Review*, 58(2): 131–143.

Rudduck, J. and McIntyre, D. (2007) *Improving Learning through Consulting Pupils*. London: Routledge.

Thomson, P. (2008) *Doing Visual Research with Children and Young People*. London: Routledge.

United Nations Convention on the Rights of the Child (1989) *UN General Assembly Resolution 44/25*. http://www2.ohchr.org/english/law/crc.htm (accessed 28th January 2010).

Vygotsky, L. S. (1978) *Mind in Society: the Development of Higher Psychological Processes*. Cambridge, MA: Harvard University Press.

Wall, K. and Higgins, S. (2006) 'Facilitating and supporting talk with pupils about meta-cognition: a research and learning tool', *International Journal of Research and Methods in Education,* 29(1): 39-53.

Worrall, S. (2000) *Young People as Researchers: a Learning Resource Pack*. London: Save the Children.

6

EXPLORING YOUR OWN AND YOUR COLLEAGUES' PROFESSIONAL KNOWLEDGE

Chapter enquiry questions

- Is the answer to your question already in your head or the head of someone else sitting in your staffroom?
- What do you and your colleagues know that you never talk about?
- How can you get at all this implicit understanding?
- What kind of question are you asking about your practice?

Introduction: What do teachers know? Making 'practical knowledge' explicit

Teachers in all contexts are experts in a series of interrelated areas of knowledge and practice: they know a great deal about learning, about classroom management, about curriculum, about ways to communicate their understanding of content and process, about the relationships with learners that promote better motivation and attainment, about the environment they work in and the communities they serve. Each teacher organises this knowledge, this collection of experience and theory, in their own unique way. The professional work of teaching does not have a single unifying theory, nor one dominant form of practice (Simon, 1999); rather, it is a patchwork of teachers' experiences, incorporating policy directives and inspection criteria alongside personal beliefs about 'good practice' and the meaning and purpose of teaching as a career (Day et al., 2006). These patchworks are strongly influenced by the institutional culture in which the teacher works and they may also be embellished by transformative experiences in the teacher's career: a challenging class or individual learner, an influential mentor or a significant learning experience in continuing professional development (Cordingley et al., 2003; 2005). Each patchwork represents an individual teacher's 'practical knowledge' or 'knowledge in action' (Wien, 1995), some of which is explicitly articulated and some of which is automatic and unexamined.

How do teachers make decisions about what to teach, when and how? How can they create a 'working space' (Leat, forthcoming) to explore what they know, what seems to be successful, and what the areas of doubt and ambiguity are? Though there is a great deal in academic literature about the importance of the 'reflective teacher' (for example, Beijaard et al., 2004), it is important to examine what it is we mean when we use this term and how reflection is used by teachers to examine their patchwork of ideas, strategies and experience and to select the best tools for each occasion. Teachers are problem solvers, constantly reacting to the needs of the learners in front of them, assessing the success of lessons or interactions and bombarded by information and competing demands. There is, therefore, a significant risk that reflection may be fragmented: short-term, narrowly focused and driven by outside agendas. Teachers may benefit from space to construct or re-evaluate a broader perspective on their work, to re-connect with their core values and purpose, but how likely is it that time will be spent in the staffroom or classroom musing, 'Why are we here?', when the immediate and pressing answer is 'To prepare for year 9 after lunch and to mark year 7's homework, to explain to Tony that conflict resolution through escalated violence is not the route advocated by the school and to make sure the bus has been booked for the field trip?'

This chapter suggests that practitioner enquiry using an action research cycle is one very effective way in which teachers can achieve reflection that is both sufficiently embedded in the day to day needs of practice and sufficiently distanced from the 'taken for granted' to be a lever for change. The structure of the chapter begins with a focus on the Teacher-researcher looking at her own practice, followed by a section on eliciting, sharing and interpreting practical knowledge with colleagues and concluding with a discussion of how enquiry can spark changes in practice across institutions.

What do you want to know about your own practice?

By undertaking an enquiry in your own classroom, you are inevitably embarking on an examination of some aspects of your own practice. What you are going to do and how you do it are key elements in the research and need to be clearly identified in your research question. (A detailed discussion of the development of your research question can be found in Chapters 3 and 4).

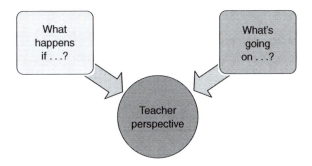

Figure 6.1   Two types of enquiry question

There are two broad types of investigation that you might undertake, depending upon whether your initial approach to action research is focused or exploratory. These can be understood in terms of whether you're asking **'what's going on?'**, which implies a descriptive exploration of interactions currently going on in your classroom; or whether you're asking **'what happens if?'**, which indicates that you are planning to make a change or series of changes and to measure their impact. Your action research project may have a 'what's happening?' phase, which generates a 'what happens if?' question, or you may begin with a focused evaluative question, which then reveals the need to look more widely at the variety of factors which influence the area you want to change.

It's perhaps obvious to say that changes in the classroom will be uneven in their effects and that it is very difficult to attribute simple cause and effect. Nevertheless, it is vital to consider this when identifying a question, particularly in relation to the **intent** of the enquiry (see Chapter 1 for a discussion of action research and intent). If you set out to change performance then the markers you look for will be in relation to that performance – be it neater handwriting, more critical questioning or scores on a maths test. You can easily generate an understanding of what change might look like. If you find these changes, having intended to cause them, it is very tempting to assume that you have indeed 'made this happen'. However, classrooms are not sealed containers and even if they were the contents are so diverse and the interactions between all the elements – the people, the ideas, the emotions, the environment – are so complex that being clear about what might be *the* cause of an observed change is almost impossible. For this reason, it is important to have elements of 'what's happening?' incorporated into the most focused of 'what happens if?' projects in order to support your awareness of this complexity.

Primary School Example

A teacher in a small (one form entry) primary school had a very focused project looking at the effect of a change in the way she taught The Victorians, using more source material and drama, on the quality and quantity of writing that her class produced. The motivation for this focus was not simply the desire to improve the writing outputs but also to inject some personal motivation for herself into a topic she had always found rather dull.

The findings from the first cycle were rather complex: children from both the higher and the lower ability groups both showed greater enjoyment and motivation and produced longer, more complex and more interesting written work than their previous performance might have predicted. However, a significant group of middle ability children appeared to find the drama work in particular distracting and the quality of their written work did not improve as much as the other groups.

In the next phase of the research cycle, the teacher audio-taped sections of her history lessons and compared them with tapes of the literacy hour; what became apparent was that her contributions in the literacy lessons offered more structure and guidelines of the connections between tasks. This led her to wonder if the improvements in history were mainly due to increased motivation and that her middle ability children's performance was more dependent on having the connections between drama and writing made more explicit, thus generating her next research question.

Tools for exploring 'what's happening?'

These kinds of research tools need to be relatively 'light touch' in terms of the time and effort spent in gathering them, since they need to be repeated over time and they need to be revisited and reviewed by the researcher. They will still require a regularity of use and a discipline in order to build up a meaningful set of data, but the reward will far outweigh the effort. Most change happens gradually and in a non-linear way, so having regular snapshots allows you to tell the story of the change realistically and rigorously.

Diaries and research logs

A research log provides a day to day record of what you *do* in a project and is an essential record of why, for example, you only have three observations from the sixth week of the project (Sarah had chicken pox) or why you decided to bring forward the post-test for the year 8s (so as not to include times when some of the classes had student teachers). Keeping an accurate research log is as much a part of good research practice as taking the register and marking work is of good teaching practice.

A research diary is something more. Ideally, it is a supplementary part of the log, so that what you are *thinking* and *feeling* are fully integrated with what you are doing. For this reason, it is important to have a book which you can carry around with you, making notes on the hoof. Better to have lots of phrases and thoughts scribbled in break time regularly than to have one or two full accounts dutifully written at a desk. When we are working with teachers engaged in action research, they sometimes put forward the view that their thoughts and feelings are not 'proper data', in the way that test scores or questionnaires are. We feel very strongly and argue passionately that this is not the case: the intention, motivation and affective states of all the people involved in the project are important aspects which have a role to play in success and failure. Throughout the book we will offer tools which may help you to tap into the thoughts and feelings of students, parents and other professionals. It is, if anything, more important to be aware of your own thoughts and feelings as the research progresses. As the designer and evaluator of the project, there is a natural tendency to see yourself as 'outside the experiment' but clearly if you teach the same lesson to one group feeling fit and energetic and then repeat it with another group with a crashing headache there may well be a different impact. There may well also be patterns in your work-ing week that you are not consciously aware of which the diary will reveal: the Wednesday afternoon slump is well-known but there are oth-ers; for example, some teachers report that they respond to an energised class coming from a PE lesson.

The research diary can also include longer observations which strike you as important during the research process: notes of group interactions, notes about behaviour, reflections upon conversations with individual students about their learning, reflections on your own role in plenary discussions. You may not have included student interviews in your research design but records of informal conversations are still useful data, giving support or challenge to your other findings. It is important to report this kind of data accurately – as unprompted informal feedback recorded in research notes, rather than as interview data – so that your research audience can make their own judgement about how to weigh it, but it is also important to include it as part of the real experience. Having a record of your thoughts, your intentions, your actions and your words to reflect upon releases you from the reliance on your memory and from the distortions of looking back from a position of knowing how it turned out. Most importantly it allows you to see how your understanding has developed over time.

Audio and video taping

The research log, supplemented by your lesson plans and assessments, gives a baseline account of what has been done in the enquiry. These are records of your intention and reports of outcomes, supplemented by your memories, and for many projects they will be sufficient. However, if you are asking a 'what's happening?' question, you may need a broader data collection tool which will scoop up the unexpected as well as the indicators you're looking for. The use of audio and video taping can be very helpful, though there are some important ethical and practical considerations to grapple with.

Video footage is classified as 'personal data' under the Data Protection Act 1998, so it is therefore essential to consider the '3 Ps': Privacy, Permission and Purpose.

Privacy	• Will the confidentiality of individuals be protected? • How will the audio or video material be securely stored?
Permission	• Do all participants have the right to opt in or out throughout the process? • Have they given permission for the data to be viewed by others?
Purpose	• Have you made the purpose of the data collection explicit? • Have you explained the ways in which the data may be used?

Figure 6.2   The 3 Ps for thinking about personal data

It is essential to comply with (or negotiate amendments to) your institution's policies in relation to the use of audio and video recording. For tips on how to use video in the classroom see Chapter 5. It may be that the use of video in your setting is covered by a generic letter signed by parents when their children start at the school or the learning agreement signed by students in the further and higher education setting, but if not you will need to get written permission for the specific purpose of gathering video evidence for research. The permission letter should reassure participants and their guardians that the video is not going to be seen by third parties (in or out of school or college), and that it will not be used for secondary purposes (for example at a conference, or using stills in a publication) without further permission being sought. There may be some learners for whom the school does not have permission to make video recordings and in such cases you need to seek advice before proceeding. It is not usually the case that these learners may not be present during video recording, but you need to consider where they are seated in relation to what the video will capture. Recordings of them speaking as part of the lesson are not restricted in the same way as visual images. Although the use of video is becoming more common in many contexts, it can still be a sensitive issue and teachers involved in research may also need reassurance about the privacy attached to the use of video evidence. This can be complicated by the power relations between the teacher being videoed and the teacher collecting the evidence – it is of critical importance to assure teachers that the video is evidence which contributes to answering your research question, not evidence of their performance, or in any way an assessment.

In practical terms, you will need to think about the kind of equipment you have access to and how that will affect your research: there are different technical problems in using either digital or analogue-recorded footage (including copying, storing, ease of use when analysing and reflecting). People do get used to being videoed, but you can expect some distraction on the first occasion, so a 'dry run' is a good idea. The less obtrusive the camera is, the better – even if that compromises some of the video quality; static cameras on tripods or filing cabinets cause less disturbance than a hand-held one. If you have a general question about interaction or process in the lesson, there is very little reason to move the camera around during the lesson, although there may be occasions when you want to capture more focused information. You need to be realistic about what you will be able to see and hear on the recording – audio quality is rarely very good and if your focus is the detailed content of student responses, you may need to have the 'belt and braces' approach of having audio recorders on the desks as well.

Audio recordings are useful if your focus is on classroom discourse. Tapes can enable you to analyse the detail both of what you say and how you say it, to count the response time you give to students or to assess the contributions and dynamics operating in collaborative groups. In the last example, there is the additional advantage of gathering data at a distance: though the presence of the recorder will have a slightly inhibiting effect on a group, this is nothing to the inhibition caused by an observer with a notebook and an eager expression.

Audio recordings have the advantage of being technically less complex than video to manage and posing fewer legal and ethical problems. However, it is still important to refer to the '3 Ps'; assure the participants and their parents that you will store the tapes securely to protect their privacy, that you will not use the recordings or transcripts to identify individuals or groups without their permission and, in general, make clear the overall purpose of the data gathering and the research project. On a practical note, check how well your microphone is working (particularly if using a separate desk mike which, as one of the authors found to her cost, needs to be switched on separately) and be aware of other environmental noise – from other groups, from heating, air conditioning and ICT equipment or in the summer from the inevitable lawnmower outside the window.

Observations by a trusted colleague

The previous section has focused on methods which are relatively self-contained in that you can manage the data collection without outside assistance. Sometimes, however, it is helpful to have another person's perspective on an interaction or approach. If that other person is a trusted colleague, with their own unique combination of skills, knowledge and experience, this can be a very fruitful source of feedback (Figure 6.3). It is better to get someone to observe in 'real time', but this is not always possible, so you may ask them to review video or audio recordings.

You need to make a distinction in your own mind and in the mind of your observer between this kind of research observation and the other kinds of peer-to-peer observation which may take place in your context for management, professional development or curriculum development purposes. Therefore, if your question is a 'what will happen if?' type, you should have a very specific set of outcomes or changes that you are looking for and your observer will be aware of them. On the other hand, a 'what's happening?' type of question might call for an observation which is very open and which doesn't have many specific parameters. In both cases, your observer's data is meant to be descriptive: what they saw and heard that seems to them to be significant in relation to your research question. Their data is not meant to be formative: this is not a coaching session intended to directly improve your performance either as a teacher or a researcher. Though there will be things you both pick up on, it is important that the observer does not engage in trying to critique your approach or to provide you with moral support; their purpose is just to give you another pair of researcher's eyes.

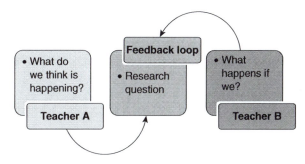

Figure 6.3   Feedback loops within peer observations

Secondary School Example

A teacher in a secondary school, engaged in a study of the impact of collaborative group work on students' understanding of scientific concepts, used audio recordings of groups at work on problem-solving and experimental activities. Her own initial analysis focused on the extent to which the groups were actually collaborating and she constructed a series of tables reflecting the amount of each individual's contribution, the length of their utterances and so on (see table below).

Looking at her data the teacher was rather disappointed that the group was dominated by Chris and Shamin and by the levels of input from the other three, whom she considered had the ability and content knowledge to make more of a contribution. She shared her concern with a colleague who offered to listen to the tape. Her take was quite different: she didn't try to count the number or length of utterances, but was struck by the high quality of the scientific language used and the relative sophistication of the discussions. She pointed out that all participants used the language and that many of the shorter contributions were taking the understanding on or introducing appropriate language (see transcript excerpt below).

> Chris: *So we've sussed that bit out, OK, now we've got to (uhmmm) look at how the thing changes, how it turns from a solid into a gas when it's heated.*
> Tara: *Sublimates*
> Chris: *Yeah, that's right. So, have we got the experiment results on the temperature and what it looked like?*

Her colleague's perspective helped the teacher to realise that group work was having an effect but that individual contributions to the process differ.

(Continued)

(Continued)

Data collection later in the project revealed that the quality of written work had increased throughout the class. The teacher concluded that there seemed to be beneficial impacts both from listening and of having listeners as a spur to better understanding.

Name	Number of utterances	Range of lengths	Mean length	Total length
Ben	14	5–25 secs	6 secs	1 min 30
Shamin	20	5 secs–1 min 25	11 secs	3 mins 40
Tara	9	5–30 secs	7 secs	1 min 4
Chris	18	20 secs – 1 min 5	11 secs	3 mins 10
Hassan	12	5–30 secs	10 secs	2 mins

Totals do not sum exactly to 11 minutes because participants talk over one another.

Although this professional learning conversation is *not* a coaching session, you can make use of the research on effective coaching practice (Lofthouse et al., 2010) to ensure that you get the most from it. There are a range of characteristics that make coaching conversations more effective and three are particularly relevant to an enquiry conversation: the intentional use of a **stimulus**, conscious movement in **scale** and awareness of the place of the conversation in **time** (see Figure 6.4 below).

As the example of the secondary teacher demonstrated, two observers can make a very different meaning from the same artefact, so it is essential for the researcher to be clear about the material used as a stimulus and for the discussion to explore the warrant: what counts as evidence and why. If the conversation takes in the underlying pedagogical aims and the context as well as the critical incident or discussion, it is likely that both parties will be able to reflect on whether the core research questions are indeed being addressed by this piece of evidence. If this is a preliminary or midcourse discussion, then there is scope for the pair to develop the research design to make it more effective but if this is a reflective look back over the enquiry, the discussion will help the researcher to understand where the strong and weak points are and to ensure that the enquiry is reported in a fair and balanced way.

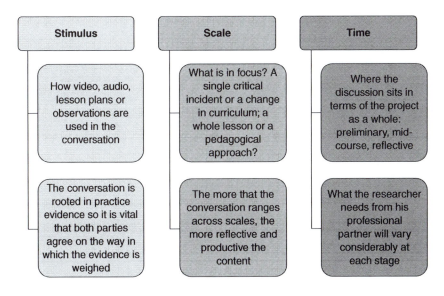

Figure 6.4   Dimensions of coaching conversations (Adapted from Lofthouse et al., 2010, p. 27)

Tools for exploring 'what happens if?'

This kind of enquiry is closer to a classic experimental design, since you are introducing a new element into your teaching and learning environment and watching for changes that you can attribute to it. Many teachers involved in action research are concerned that their enquiry is not sufficiently 'scientific' if they do not have control groups or if the comparison classes are not precisely matched to the experimental ones. The issue for us is one of clarity: the rigour and validity of your enquiry rests on how well you report what you have done and how much weight you place on your findings. For example, to report that 'Achievement in maths rose by 20%' it needs to be contextualised (see Table 6.1 below for a few possible examples) – clearly the kind of measure and comparison is dependent on the focus of your original research question.

Ipsative (self-referenced) comparisons are commonly used in classroom enquiry, since the driver for your project is likely to be improving outcomes for your students. It is perfectly valid to report the gains that your students have made and to make reference to how far they have exceeded your predictions (if applicable) provided that you do not, even implicitly, claim that your intervention has definitely been the factor which made this difference. If you are doing a peer comparison, it is important to include as much information as possible about how similar or different

Table 6.1   Contextualising data

Achievement in maths rose by 20%	Compared to?	Based on?	Over time?
Ipsative (group)	Previous performance of this group	Scores on maths test	One term
Ipsative (individual)	Individual performances	Scores on homework assignments	Two terms
Comparative (cohort)	Last year's Year 6	SATs results	Snapshot
Comparative (peer)	The other Year 6 class who didn't do the intervention	SATs results	One year

the groups are and, for a cohort comparison, whether there were significant factors in the previous year(s) such as building work disruption, staff changes or a greater than normal change in learner movement which could have had an impact. Peer or cohort comparisons will allow you to make slightly stronger claims about your intervention's role in the observed improvement, though you should be wary of attributing simple cause and effect.

The case study from Wilbury Primary School (below) shows how the use of comparison classes can be used to support the project's ipsative findings.

To What Extent is the Development of Speaking and Listening Skills a Prerequisite for Children to Become More Efficient Learners?

Ann Mulcahy and Elaine Saini

Wilbury Primary School, Enfield

PROJECT AIMS

This research project aims to explore the hypothesis that the development of speaking and listening skills improves the children's attitudes to learning, behaviour and their capacity to evaluate their learning.

Writing sample completed by below average boy in October 2003

RESEARCH PROCESS

We realised that a key factor necessary for success was the development of the children's ability to talk about how, as well as what, they were learning. This led to the primary focus being a specific development of speaking and listening. We ensured that observational evidence, including that from the learners themselves, was collected early on and throughout the year. This was in addition to the continued use of learner templates and analysis of attainment and behavioural data.

A programme of skills to encourage talk and to improve the quality of paired work and feedback was undertaken with the project class of Year 3 children while the other three Year 3 classes acted as a comparison group.

Positive, supportive paired relationships had developed over the year, with a reduction in negative comments and a greater understanding of how to work together, evidenced by their own accounts and Learner Views Templates. Children of all ability levels were found to be using sentences of greater length and of greater complexity by the year's end. The children were

(Continued)

(Continued)

also able to complete observations of one another's talk and to identify key features of feedback.

At the start of the year the project class was seen as the class with the lowest attainment as adjudged by the SATs results, yet by the end they were the class who had made the most progress.

	Project Class [30 children]	Comparison Classes [90 children]
Reading	5.6	2.2
Writing	5.4	3.3
Mathematics	2.5	2.0

FINDINGS

- The strategies used improved children's speaking and listening skills as well as giving them the language and ability to talk about their own learning.
- There would seem to be a clear link between this development of speaking and listening and the raising of attainment.
- The development of a positive ethos within the class, inherent in the L2L approach, may have supported improvements in the children's behaviours.
- Underlying any of these successful outcomes was the need for the teacher to be knowledgeable, enthusiastic and committed to L2L approaches.

(For full details of the project please see http://www.campaignforlearning. org.uk/)

For all of these approaches it is important to take early 'baseline' measures using testing or observations: the earlier, the better. Even if you have not finalised your research question, a general observation or video taken early in the year can be re-analysed to yield specific data about behaviours, questioning or group processes later on. Similarly, broadly focused tests of ability which you would probably do with a new group as part of ongoing planning and assessment can do a double duty as baseline research data. A particular advantage of early baselining is that you have the maximum gap between your pre- and post-tests: since change can take some time to embed and become 'visible' to testing, you are giving yourself a greater chance to measure the effects.

An important consideration is the number of repeat tests or observations you plan to complete and this will, in part, depend on how complex or onerous your research tools are to complete and analyse (see Chapter 5 for an extended discussion of learner observation tools). However, the rate of change and the kinds of change that happen will differ according to your focus: it is likely that for an enquiry with a strong attainment or outcome focus you will need fewer repeat measures than for an enquiry which is exploring process, motivation or behaviour. If you do undertake a series of observations, it is vital that you include an element of personal reflection: are you absolutely clear about what you are observing and the characteristics you are using to define it and are you aware of how much you are impacting on the observation?

Primary School Example

Two relatively inexperienced researchers were working in a school as part of a project looking at classroom discourse and spent a morning in Year 5 classes, observing plenaries in the Literacy Hour and coding the teacher's questions. Henry enthused that his session included lots of open questions, while Joe bemoaned the fact that there were hardly any in his. Later the project team conducted an exercise in inter-rater reliability, where everyone watched the videos of the plenaries and coded the questions. The more experienced team members' coding differed, but not very widely, and tended to rate both classes as having similar levels of open questions. As the discussion developed, it became clear that Henry had been basing his coding on his interpretation of the *teacher's intent* when asking the question and Joe was using his assessment of the *learners' response*. The vexing question of what an open question actually might be is still being addressed elsewhere (Smith and Higgins, 2006) though, in the meantime, the team developed a tighter working definition.

What do you want to find out about other teachers?

You may have a research question which goes beyond your own practice or your own classroom: you may be engaged in a collaborative enquiry across a curriculum team or within a year group or key stage, or your question might be focused more upon variations in professional practice. These questions draw upon our understanding of shared expertise and can help us to make more explicit the communities of practice (Lave and Wenger, 1991) which operate in our contexts.

If your research question is focused on the way other teachers approach a particular area of practice – a 'what's happening elsewhere?' question – then one of your key research tools will be observation. All of the considerations discussed earlier apply, with the additional factor of your role as observer and the power relations between you and the teachers that you are observing. It is self-evident that a teacher will have a different view of you coming into her classroom to observe (or watching a video of her practice) depending on whether you are relatively junior to her and apparently 'watching to learn' or relatively senior to her and 'watching to critique'. The key to overcoming these natural fears is absolute clarity about the intent of your project, the focus of the research and the role that the observation will play. Only then can the teacher give informed consent to being involved and ethical principles demand that this is the only form of consent that is good enough.

Higher Education Example

A colleague from another university planned to do his doctoral research on the immortal question 'What makes a lecturer funny?' but he was aware that his pragmatic plan to recruit colleagues from his Faculty would carry with it all kinds of potential problems. Peer observation is an established practice in his context but he knew that everyone tried to be on 'best behaviour' even when there was no obvious inspection or management agenda. This was going to be problematic for him, since he was hoping to catch humour: both the planned and the spontaneous would need his colleagues to be relaxed. He knew that he was never going to entirely 'get around' this issue but he re-organised his enquiry so that his focus groups came before his observations. This meant that all the participants had an opportunity to discuss the key issues of humour in teaching and to think through the meaning of their participation in the project before the observations. Though we cannot know for sure, the rich data and the large numbers of good jokes are an indication that this was a useful strategy.

More approaches to finding out what other teachers know

Ideally, observations and other data from your colleagues will be explored and enriched through the use of other qualitative methods such as questionnaires, focus groups and individual interviews. A detailed discussion of questionnaire design can be found in Chapter 7 but some special consideration to giving questionnaires to colleagues needs to be addressed here. It is tempting to assume that the purpose of your enquiry is self-evident and to ask very open-ended questions which require a great deal of writing. This can often backfire in two ways: busy teachers will be reluctant to compose essays about their teaching and the data you do get back will be individual, idiosyncratic and difficult to analyse. Questionnaire design should be extremely focused and aim to elicit mainly factual (how much, how often, when in the term/year?) information. This can then serve as a foundation to explore the more complex questions of which relate to motivation (why this and not another, why at all?) and affect (how does this feel, how do they react?) which are more easily tackled through interviews and focus groups. Questions of time and focus are equally important here: ask yourself how much spare time you have in an average working day. With this in mind, a good rule of thumb is a maximum of two sides of an A4 sheet for questionnaires, and an interview or focus group schedule should have no more than five focused questions or one open question and should not be scheduled to last more than an hour. Audio recording is extremely helpful for both interviews and focus groups, as it allows you to be fully engaged in the conversation and to support and extend the discussion without being distracted by note taking. Video of focus groups can be useful in identifying individual speakers but if your focus is on exploring a range of views, rather than attributing those views to individuals, it is probably not worth the bother.

Individual interviews enable you to explore issues in depth and afford your interviewee a confidential, safe space to talk about his practice; focus groups will give you a range of views, enable you to map complementary and opposing views together and have the advantage of many brains attacking the same problem. Both have disadvantages: individual interviews are time consuming to conduct and to analyse; focus groups are vulnerable to being hijacked by the most articulate or opinionated participants. Whichever approach you choose, it is good practice to engage your colleagues as co-enquirers rather than research subjects. Always share your interview or group questions beforehand so that people come prepared and engaged, and give them a reasonable proportion of the time to suggest other questions or means of approaching the problem. The quality of your data will be immeasurably improved by your recognition of their expert status and you will be contributing to a culture of mutual support and collaborative working within your context.

In a collaborative enquiry, it is vital to have regular, protected time in which to meet and discuss the progress of the research, the particular problems and techniques associated with different tools and the emerging understanding of the problem. The support of the management team in your context will be needed to give your work the necessary status to 'carve out' this protected time. One of the most common reasons for collaborative enquiries to be less successful is a lack of institutional support.

In our experience of working with teachers engaged in practitioner enquiry we have become aware of a variety of processes which seem to support the development of a community of enquirers. In the initial phases, individual teachers or small groups begin to work on classroom-based projects. They have limited contact with one another about this, often only at the end of a cycle, when findings are shared across the institution. This distributed network can offer a level of support and encouragement, but it lacks formal recognition from senior management and the onus is on the teachers themselves to share their learning about the process of research, good and bad research tools and the difficulties and triumphs of analysis.

Over time, however, the individuals and groups begin to form a more coherent identity, often with the support of an advocate of enquiry from the management team. Their work becomes less of a fringe activity: they may have more resources and support in terms of time or cover to conduct their research; indeed some institutions give bursaries to individuals or groups to support teacher research. This, of course, makes research a more attractive prospect for other colleagues and they join in until the institution finds itself at a 'tipping point' where sufficient numbers of staff are so involved that research is a mainstream activity, which permeates CPD, staff meetings, curriculum development and forward planning. The feedback loops from individual enquiries begin to join up, creating a community of enquirers who can learn from and support one another. Sometimes bigger research projects emerge, though this does not mean that larger enquiries drive out the smaller ones: the individual teacher's autonomy in choosing her focus is the engine which keeps the community ticking over.

Key perspectives on exploring professional knowledge

The context of your own and your colleagues' professional knowledge is an important factor, since the life history of teachers and the circumstances in which they work shape the ways in which they take in, process and adapt new learning.

Cochran-Smith, M. and Lytle, S.L. (2004) 'Practitioner Inquiry, Knowledge and University Culture', in J.J. Loughran, M.L. Hamilton, V.K. LaBoskey and T.L. Russell (eds), *International Handbook of Self-Study of Teaching and Teacher Education Practices*. Dordrecht: Kluwer Academic Publishers.

Frost, D. and Durrant, J. (2003) *Teacher-Led Development Work*. London: David Fulton.
Nias, J. (1989) *Primary Teachers Talking: a Study of Teaching as Work*. London: Routledge.

References used in this chapter

Beijaard, D., Meijer, P.C. and Verloop, N. (2004) 'Reconsidering research on teachers' professional identity', *Teaching and Teacher Education*, 20(2): 107–128.

Cordingley, P., Bell, M., Evans, D. and Firth, A. (2005) *The impact of collaborative CPD on classroom teaching and learning: What do teacher impact data tell us about collaborative CPD?* London: EPPI-Centre.

Cordingley, P., Bell, M., Rundell, B., Evans, D. and Curtis, A. (2003) *The impact of collaborative CPD on classroom teaching and learning: How does collaborative Continuing Professional Development (CPD) for teachers of the 5–16 age range affect teaching and learning?* London: EPPI-Centre.

Day, C., Stobart, G., Sammons, P. and Kington, A. (2006) 'Variations in the work and lives of teachers: relative and relational effectiveness', *Teachers and Teaching: Theory and Practice*, 12: 169–192.

Lave, J. and Wenger, E. (1991) *Situated Learning: Legitimate Peripheral Participation.* Cambridge: Cambridge University Press.

Lofthouse, R., Leat, D. and Towler, C. (2010) *Coaching for Teaching and Learning: a Practical Guide for Schools.* Reading: CfBT Education Trust.

Simon, B. (1999) 'Why no pedagogy in England?', in J. Leach and B. Moon (eds), *Learners and Pedagogy.* London: Paul Chapman/Open University: 34–45.

Smith, H. and Higgins, S.E. (2006) 'Opening classroom interaction: the importance of feedback', *Cambridge Journal of Education*, 36(4): 485–502.

Wien, C.A. (1995) *Developmentally Appropriate Practice in 'Real Life': Stories of Teacher Practical Knowledge.* New York: Teachers College Press.

7

ENGAGING WITH THE VIEWS OF FAMILIES AND THE WIDER COMMUNITY

Chapter enquiry questions

- What can you learn from parents and carers?
- What sort of questions normally get asked and how?
- How can this communication be made more interesting and complex?
- Can communication with families become part of ongoing cycles of enquiry?

Introduction: accessing data beyond the school gates

It will hardly be news to any teacher that the impact of individual schools on children's outcomes is by far outweighed by factors relating to the area they live in (HEFCE, 2005), the ethnicity (Mirza, 2006; Harding, 2006) and socio-economic status of the family, the educational background of the parents and other children in the family (Sacker et al., 2002) and the attitude of the family towards education and the child's achievement (Desforges and Abouchaar, 2003). The last of these factors – family attitudes and support for learning – is at the same time one of the most powerful (Hattie, 2009) *and* the only one that schools can realistically engage with. Philosophers and politicians argue that education is an agent for economic and social change but what teachers and schools can achieve does not include the economic regeneration of areas. Rather, we have to work with communities and families *as they are* and develop ways of communicating so that the goals and aspirations of home and school come closer together and develop dynamically over time.

Many teachers engaged in enquiry have designed questions which are tightly focused on curriculum, classroom interaction and assessing the quality and extent of students' understanding, and for this reason they do not tend to include collecting data from parents or including parents in the reflection process. When the research cycle is repeated, however, many teachers find that they need this perspective to make sense of their data. To put it in experimental terms, the classroom is not a closed system and any change that is made and evaluated in the classroom needs to take some account of the factors which, while not physically present, have a considerable effect on interactions and outcomes.

> When we looked at our first year results, there seemed to be differences between the children [in performance] that we couldn't explain by looking at their old test scores or their general behaviour and attitude in class. We had sent support materials home and we wondered if that had made the difference – some parents using them, some not. When we asked some of the parents we found that they had mostly been using the games but had really different ideas about what they were for – some of them really good ideas, just different from ours! This year, we're trying to get the parents involved at the beginning, so we're all singing from the same sheet.
> (Key Stage 2 Maths project)

Including parents in your thinking about the action research cycle means taking some time at the outset to explore what you know about parents, what constitutes a reasonable and achievable question or set of questions and how you are going to evaluate the responses that you get, in the same way as you have done before. However, there is a further layer when dealing with parents or the wider community: you have to make a distinction between research purposes. These commonly divide between *validating* the work you have already done with children, *recruiting* parents to the teaching and learning team and *exploring* parents' perspectives (Figure 7.1).

In validation research, you are essentially asking '*How did we do?*'. You need to present your target group of parents with plenty of information about your work in the classroom – not just what you have done but what your underlying intentions are – and provide them with a range of ways to respond to it. You can often do validation after the event, though the data you get will be richer if you start sharing information at the beginning and you will have the opportunity to sample parents' opinions at different points in the process. The tools you'll use will probably be quite focused and may include structured questionnaires or surveys.

In recruiting projects, you are asking parents to become active partners in the business of teaching and learning, asking, '*What can we do together?*' The intervention itself involves parents supporting their child's learning through participation at home or at school and will be evaluated through a mixture of methods: the impact on learning or behaviour in school, the reported feelings of students and parents and the quality of communication between parents and teachers. Attainment data, behaviour or attendance records and questionnaire or interview data will be complementary tools in this sort of project.

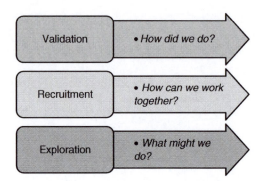

Figure 7.1   Ways to include parents in the action research cycle

In exploratory research, you are fundamentally asking, '*What might we do?*' Often this represents the next stage in teacher's thinking about working with parents. An initiative may have been validated and had an observable impact on most parents in one year but then have been less successful the next. Alternatively, some parents loved it but others disliked or ignored it – it boils down to the fact that the answers you got from asking '*How did we do?*' weren't simple or satisfactory; instead you may need to find out about the underlying expectations that you and the parents have, to work out how you can get together to achieve the goals of the research. You'll need more open-ended research tools like focus groups and interviews and the role of parents in the process tends to be more active: some of them may come to be 'research partners'.

What do you already know about parents?

Schools collect a lot of information and ask for a lot of feedback, directly and indirectly. Every report that goes home, every letter asking for comments and responses, every open meeting is an opportunity for the school to gather information about parents – their situations, their views, their priorities for their children.

You already know a lot about parents' ideas about the school, though it may not be explicit knowledge. For example, you know whether parents come in to talk to you informally or whether they come in only at your request or theirs to deal with specific issues. This will, in part, be shaped by the policies in your school and the age of children you teach but it is also a piece of information about what your parents think is appropriate in terms of communication. You will also be able to compare your experiences with those of your colleagues – do certain age groups, subject areas or roles within the school attract more contact between home and school? This is particularly important information if you want to increase the levels of communication, since you can be strategic, building on from where relationships are already strong. It is also interesting to canvass your colleagues' opinions about parents: are home–school relationships generally good? Are there specific groups of parents who are more or less 'on-side' than others? Do some kinds of events attract more parents than others? You may be surprised about the diversity of answers you get, even in a small school, but it is important to explore what the school's assumptions about parents are. It may be useful to check up on how the school communicates with parents: do some letters look more 'official' than others? How many times a year are parents asked for information or opinions already and what are the response rates like? This will save you time asking for repeated information and enable you to think critically about how to approach your research question.

You will know, or be able to find out, how many hits your school website gets, how quickly parents sign up for parents' evening meetings and how often these meetings over-run, or how many people are actively involved in volunteering in the school, or – by going through the contact information for your students – you may be able to estimate how many parents are working, or how many students are cared for by the extended family. This could be vital information if you are wanting to have conversations in your project about homework support, for example.

Ways of organising and adding to this data

As far as possible, you need to work with the existing systems used in your school, though some of these will probably be held as electronic files, which will make life easier. Setting up monitoring systems *in advance* for homework completion, library books, story sack borrowing or other activities will enable you and other colleagues to gather ongoing data easily. Make good use of the school calendar, so that you have plenty of notice of events where parents will be accessible to you, such as assemblies, open evenings and school fairs, and can plan surveys, questionnaires or focus groups to coincide with them. It is important to spend some time making sure that your data about parents is of reasonable quality: for example, working from an old address list will significantly impact on the number of questionnaire responses you get. When talking to your colleagues, keep an informal note of parents they mention as supportive – these people can be key partners in designing your questions or recruiting other parents.

Feedback loops

As we discuss throughout this book, one of the principal benefits of practitioner enquiry is the creation of feedback loops for the teacher about teaching and learning as it happens. The feedback loops between home and school vary in size and efficacy because of a range of factors relating to the age of the students, the culture of the school and the relationships between teachers and parents. However, even the twice-daily feedback between parent and teacher in a nursery setting, for example, could be *focused* and *enhanced* by the structure of a research project. Sharing information with parents about an enquiry and seeking regular feedback throughout the project can improve the research questions, re-focus the data collection and inform the analysis.

Doing validation research with parents

This takes your classroom-based action research to a more sophisticated level, recognising the importance of the learning and experience that children have outside of school and exploring the extent to which parents can track changes in children's learning or behaviour and triangulate your own findings.

Infant School Example

A year one class has been using Community of Enquiry techniques throughout the spring term to encourage higher order thinking in science and to encourage children to make and support hypotheses about growing plants. The teacher has research data which shows that more than half of the children are talking about plant growth in a more logical and systematic way, that they are able to debate possibilities with one another and that the format of Community of Enquiry appears to be encouraging a small group

---

of children, previously reluctant to speak in large group situations, to make a significantly larger number of contributions. The teacher had sent topic information to parents in September but had not given specific information about the research project or about Community of Enquiry. She conducted a number of informal interviews with parents during the tea and coffee session after the class assembly (on *The Enormous Sunflower*), where she asked them if the children had talked about the science topic at home. She received a certain amount of validation from some of these conversations, but was surprised to learn that several parents mentioned that they felt their children were exhibiting some challenging behaviours at home, particularly using the formula '*I disagree with that because* …'. An animated discussion sprang up between a group of parents about this, with some expressing concern about 'cheeky' behaviour and others showing pride in the child's 'feisty' stance.

As this example demonstrates, it is important to keep an open mind about the potential impact of an intervention which has specific aims within the classroom but which may produce other results in different contexts. The teacher in this case realised that because she had not made either the purpose or the processes of Community of Enquiry explicit to the parents, children were getting quite variable feedback from home. Moreover, the feedback she was asking for from parents was not based on a shared understanding of what was being evaluated – what change was intended and how it might look or sound.

Useful tools for validation

Short questionnaires

Short questionnaires are a good research tool for repeated use: if your enquiry is tracking changes in behaviour which might be observed at home as well as at school, a short questionnaire can be used to create a baseline and be repeated at the end of the project, or at intervals, to track gradual change. When you are asking parents about behaviours, it is a good idea to avoid '*always, frequently, sometimes, rarely, never*' headings for responses, since these are ambiguous: my 'sometimes' could be a lot less than yours. Specific measures, '*more than twice a day, every day, two or three times a week, once a week, less than once a week*', are easier to understand and also give you a better basis for comparison. A project which reports that before the intervention '*most parents "sometimes" talked about maths at home with their children but afterwards the proportion of those who "frequently" did so rose by a third'* sounds OK but being able to say *'Before the project only 25% of parents said they talked about maths every day and 15% said they talked about it less than once a week. After the "Maths is Everywhere" project, 48% said they talked about maths every day and all parents talked about maths at least once a week'* is both a lot clearer and more impressive.

Short questionnaires are also useful for gathering descriptive data about parents' current ideas or practice. In general, the questions should be clear, short and, where possible, allow the respondent to tick a box rather than write a long answer. It is important that the questionnaire does not ask for information you already have or that does not seem relevant to the research question. For example, a project focusing on reading and looking at reading homework might justifiably ask about the range of adults who spend time caring for the child after school, though it would be important to look carefully at the phrasing of the question. Comparing the two examples below, which would you react best to?

Do you help your child with their reading homework?

Every night   Most nights   Some nights   Never

If you don't read every night, does someone else do it?

(please specify) _____

We are looking at how best to organise the reading homework for Class 5. Please fill in the table below so we know what you and your child are doing after school

	Monday	Tuesday	Wednesday	Thursday	Friday
Child looked after by e.g. Mum, Dad, Grandparent, Childminder, After school club					
Other after school activities e.g. Cubs, Brownies, music, sport, other clubs, helping at home					
Good days for reading homework are					

Figure 7.2   Two examples of questionnaire question formats for parents

If you are looking for parents' views, you can give them a series of positive and negative statements, to which they can either agree/disagree or give a range of responses on a Likert scale (for example, *Strongly Agree, Agree, Neither Agree or Disagree, Disagree, Strongly Disagree)*. However, we would recommend that you draw these statements from interviews or focus groups (see below) that you have carried out with a smaller group of parents in the school, since it may be a mistake to assume that you can guess what the range of views might be.

A good rule of thumb for a short questionnaire is that it should fit on one side of an A4 sheet and be quick to fill in. Bear in mind that if you want to repeat the questionnaire and want to track changes in individuals you will not be able to make them anonymous, though you can give each family a number so that you are not focusing on what you *think* you know about them when you are looking at responses. If you use anonymous question-naires you will only be able to track changes in the cohort as a whole and if you don't get all of them back, you won't necessarily know if you're com-paring the same twenty responses from before and after. However, if you're looking at opinions and not planning to repeat, you may find that you get more responses if parents know they are responding anonymously.

Home–school learner logs

Home–school learner logs are a particularly good research tool if you want to set up regular feedback and to develop conversations with parents about learning. As the examples below show, they can be used with very

Today at school I

It made me feel ☹ ☺ ☺ because

Today at home I

It made me feel ☹ ☺ ☺ because

Figure 7.3   Two examples of home–school learner logs, one completely unstructured, one with a basic drawing structure and a focus on affective and motivational data collection

As learners get older, the focus of feedback can be more specific and can be used to make parents aware of the demands or the language being used in the classroom.

Figure 7.4   Two examples of learner logs designed for older students, emphasising process and intention within lessons and making explicit links to metacognition

young learners as a way of sharing experiences, using drawings, collage or photographs. However, they have their uses with older learners too, as the case study example used in Chapter 1 from a university dental school demonstrates.

Informal interviews and focus groups

This is probably the most efficient method of gauging parents' opinions, since the organisation of the interviews or focus group is ideally 'piggy-backed' onto a pre-existing event when parents are available, such as an assembly, open evening or sports event. Teachers in primary settings can also experiment with having more flexible time boundaries for parents at the beginning and end of the day, for example having an 'open' story-time to which parents are welcomed, or a collaborative first activity of the day at which parents can stay and participate. Be aware, however, that you are only accessing a limited sample of parents and carers at these events: you will be much less likely to encounter those working full time, for example. You will find it a great advantage if you can offer tea or coffee and biscuits to encourage parents to come and linger and to have a 'briefing sheet' about your enquiry project that parents can look at. Limit yourself to one area of data collection and, if possible, to one key and focused question that parents can reasonably be expected to respond to without preparation. It is far more comfortable for parents to be asked, *'Does Tom like the new reading scheme better than the old one?'* – a question that they can easily answer and which may then lead on to them discussing related topics about books, reading and their child, than to be asked, *'We're putting more emphasis on phonics in our teaching this term – have you noticed a difference in the way Tom spells out words?'* – a question which parents might want to know about in advance, so that they could watch for the change.

Longer questionnaires

Sometimes it is necessary to ask quite a lot of questions of parents. In that case a longer questionnaire, with a mixture of open and closed questions is advisable. Even with a longer format, it is important to make sure that the layout is clear and the categories are relatively unambiguous. If possible, keep the questionnaire to less than four sides and print on both sides of the paper so that parents don't feel they have a huge sheaf of paper to deal with. The example below was created with the teachers at Lanner school in Cornwall as part of the *Learning to Learn* project.

Recruiting parents to collaborative projects

Teachers have long recognised the benefits of engaging parental support for learning, either through homework support, positive encouragement and active modelling in schools through volunteering. In collaborative projects, the aim is for parents and schools to work together towards a common goal (for further detail on participatory approaches see Chapter 4). It is very important to make sure that the project is set up in such a way as to enable parents to have some input into the 'goal setting'. While teachers may identify an area in which they want to target children's motivation and learning, it is an advantage to involve parents early on in the planning stages, rather than presenting them with activities and ideas in a way which could be perceived as patronising. Even if this is not practically possible, the ways in which parents are invited to take part are crucial – avoiding the impression of singling out families of children who are 'struggling', not portraying the parents' role as 'teacher's helper' and, more positively, valuing the perspectives of parents.

Lanner Parent Questionnaire

About your child's learning at school

1. How confident are you that you know what your child is learning at school? *Please tick one box*

Not at all confident	I know some of what is going on	I know most of what is going on	Very confident

2. How do you find out what your child is learning at school? *Please tick all that apply*

The school send me letters and leaflets	My child tells me	My child's teacher tells me	I hear about things from other parents	Other (please state below)

Other ways of finding out_____

3. How confident are you that you understand how your child is learning at school? *Please tick one box*

Not at all confident	I know some of what is going on	I know most of what is going on	Very confident

4. How do you find out how your child is learning at school? *Please tick all that apply*

The school send me letters and leaflets	My child tells me	My child's teacher tells me	I hear about things from other parents	Other (please state below)

Other ways of finding out_____

5. Would you be interested in finding out more about what and how your child is learning at school? *Please tick one box*

Yes	No

6. What sort of information or event would you find useful? *Please tick all that apply*

Visiting the school/ watching lessons	Meetings with teachers	After-school events on subjects and learning approaches	More information to read at home	Other (please state below)

Other information / event_____

About your child's learning at home

7. Do you agree with the statement "Learning only takes place at school"? *Please tick one box*

Yes	No

8. Does homework help your child to reinforce his/her learning? *Please tick one box*

A lot	Quite a lot	It depends on the subject (please go to Q.9)	Not very much	Not at all

9. How much does homework help your child to reinforce their learning? *Please tick one box*

	A lot	Quite a lot	Not very much	Not at all
Reading				
Writing				
Maths				
Topic work				

10. Do you help your child with homework? *Please tick one box*

Always	Quite a lot	Not very much	Not at all

11. Do you agree with the statement "Children should do their homework independently"? *Please tick one box*

Yes	No

12. Do you agree with the statement "Parents can help their children's learning in a different way from teachers?" *Please tick one box*

Yes	No

13. Is your child motivated to complete their homework? *Please tick one box*

Always	Most of the time	Sometimes	Rarely

14. If your child is less motivated sometimes, why do you think this is? *Please tick all that apply*

Bored with school work	Too busy with other activities	Too tired after school	Homework too hard	Homework too easy	Other (please state)

Other _____

15. Do you have any other concerns or ideas about learning in our school that you would like to raise? *Please use this space to let us know.*

Figure 7.5 Example of a longer questionnaire for parents

These points are illustrated by the following two case study examples, one from a primary and one from a secondary school. Both of these are good examples of the way in which working together with parents enables a common language about learning and assessment to build up, which then provides better support for students and shows itself in higher levels of motivation, engagement and attainment.

Does Introducing Parents to Learning to Learn Techniques have a Positive Effect on Pupils' Achievement?

Linda Stephens and Irene Pooley

St Meriadoc C of E Infant School, Cornwall

PROJECT AIMS

We are looking at the role of family learning in supporting Learning to Learn by arranging a series of evenings to introduce parents to the major L2L approaches. We will monitor the impact that the parents' involvement has on the confidence and capability of their children.

RESEARCH PROCESS

We decided to hold a series of 9 sessions for parents. These were held in the school hall every fortnight starting in October and continuing into the Spring Term. We agreed that the best time to hold the meetings was in the evenings so that more people would have a chance of attending.

An initial invitation was sent out which included a paragraph about our involvement in the Campaign for Learning Research Project. We made it clear that although it was not necessary to attend all sessions we would be keeping a register of parents so that we could see whether regular attendance had more effect that just coming to one or two talks.

The topics covered were:

1 Seeing yourself as a learner, which included self-talk and neuro-linguistic programming (NLP).
2 Three main ways to learn, VAK and brain gym.
3 Overcoming barriers to learning by raising self-esteem.
4 Memory skills and techniques to aid memory.
5 Visual learning including mind maps.
6 The different ways of being intelligent, a brief overview of all of the intelligences.
7 Thinking skills, various ways of promoting thinking e.g. by odd-one-out puzzles, mysteries, fortune lines.
8 The importance of talk, in particular using a 'philosophy with children' approach.
9 Formative assessment and reflecting on your own learning.

(Continued)

(Continued)

At the end of each session parents were encouraged to note down anything that they felt they had learnt from that particular session or general comments about how they thought it had gone. At the end of the series of talks parents were issued with a questionnaire to determine how they felt their attendance would benefit their children's learning.

FINDINGS

We found out that:

- Sharing Learning to Learn approaches with parents raises their own self-esteem and confidence as learners.
- Involving parents in Learning to Learn enables them to feel more able to teach and help their own children at home.
- The confidence of the parents communicates itself to the children.
- Even after only a few months, improvements have been noticed in some of the children's performance.

Assessing the Impact of 'Getting Parents More Involved in School' Programme on Student Motivation and Attainment

John Welham

Camborne Science and Community College, Cornwall

PROJECT AIMS

The project aims to evaluate the impact of a programme, in which parents of Year 11 GCSE students were invited to school sessions in and out of school time. The project seeks to involve parents more directly in the work of their children at school in order to sustain and develop student motivation and thus improve attainment.

RESEARCH PROCESS

Parents were invited to join their children and the Design Technology teachers for two introductory sessions, where they were given the outline of the course and a breakdown of the coursework assignments. They were then introduced to five things that the staff promised to do and five things that students would need to do, before being given a list of five things they could do that would help their children to complete the coursework successfully. This included simple suggestions such as talking to their child about the coursework assignment; making time each week to review their progress; contacting school if they had any concerns; agreeing to support their children's attendance at out-of-hours sessions.

Parents were then shown an exhibition of selected (successful) samples of the previous year's coursework and the breakdown of the grades for those pieces of coursework.

The parents of just over 80% of the students involved in the project attended this first session.

The next stage was to invite these parents to a DT lesson during school time. They attended a special session, with their children, which modelled the coursework process and helped them to understand how their children were expected to work.

Finally, there was a celebration of coursework evening, open to the whole school community, to which the parents and students were invited.

GCSE coursework scores in Design and Technology and Geography from previous years and GCSE coursework scores, hand-in and completion rates from Design and Technology groups not involved in the project – for comparison data – were collected.

Before and after the intervention, data about student performance was collected, including GCSE coursework scores in DT from previous years, GCSE coursework scores and completion rates. Colleagues were interviewed as a follow-up measure, while parents and students were interviewed throughout the life of the project and when the coursework was completed.

FINDINGS

This enquiry found:

- The intervention seems to have had a distinct impact on coursework marks, which in turn has impacted on GCSE grades attained.
- Feedback from teachers, students and teachers has been very positive.

Advocacy

Often another goal of projects like these is that groups of parents will act as advocates, drawing in less engaged groups of parents into school activities and creating a wider learning network around the school. This is a process that takes a significant amount of time and relies heavily on the personal qualities of the teachers and parents involved, so it is vital not to have too high an expectation of this kind of effect in the early years of a project.

Research suggests that the more similar the home and school cultures are, the easier it is to get widespread engagement in a relatively short time (e.g. Hall and Santer, 2000). However, in all schools, the population of families constantly changes and it is important to consider outreach and advocacy elements of parental involvement as continually evolving.

Useful tools for collaborative projects

The tools for validation research are equally valid in collaborative projects, in particular the use of learning logs to keep dialogue between home and school ticking over throughout the project. In reflecting on the experience of working together, the use of reasonably short and structured **interviews** is a particularly useful strategy. It may well not be practical to interview all the parents in the project and you will have to decide what criteria you will use to construct a sub-sample. You may have been collecting other data – for example on pupil attainment or confidence – which will provide you with a sampling frame (see example below). This will enable you to talk to a representative group of parents.

Table 7.1 Sampling frame for working with parents

Example sampling frame	Children with higher confidence scores	Children with medium confidence scores	Children with lower confidence scores
Parents involved	(Total=5) **2**	(Total=6) **2**	(Total=2) **1**
Parents not involved	(Total=4) **2**	(Total=7) **2**	(Total=3) **1**

You may not have data that is suitable for creating a sampling frame, but you may have conducted a questionnaire, which will allow you to pick out parents with a range of perspectives to explore in more detail in the interviews. Or you may not really know what the issues are for parents and will have to conduct an opportunity sample, where you ask parents to volunteer to discuss the project with you and you work with perhaps a single open question asking them to reflect on their experiences. This is a harder approach to manage, because you can only judge when to stop doing interviews when you feel that your research categories from the interviews are 'saturated': that you are not getting any new data from parents.

Interviews need to take place in a quiet space, away from distractions and interruptions, at a time when neither you nor your interviewee has to be somewhere else urgently and can relax and give full attention to the interaction. Again, tea and biscuits are helpful. The interview questions should be shared in advance of the interview, so that there is no feeling of surprise or discomfort. The design of a short interview schedule needs to have no more than five focused questions for a half hour interview, particularly if you intend to keep to time. A single, reflective, open question can work equally well in this situation.

Working with parents to generate research questions

Exploratory projects are often features of the second or third cycle of action research. Previous exploration has thrown up a series of questions, some of them the 'bigger' questions, like '*Why do Year 10s suddenly become unwilling to accept public praise?*' or '*How much do we need to know about how children have slept and eaten in order to assess how ready they are to learn in the morning?*' Teachers may have reached a point where they are unsure which is the 'right', or indeed the most relevant, research question. Schools may wish to engage in consultation with parents about their strengths and weaknesses as part of self-evaluation and the quest for continuous improvement.

For any and all of these reasons, exploratory research projects arise. There are two key elements: getting a broad spectrum of opinion and getting an in-depth understanding of those opinions. These are potentially in conflict, so it is important to get a feedback cycle built into the design from the start. For example, an exploratory research project might start with the report of a successful Ofsted inspection. The report is circulated to all parents, together with a letter which draws their attention to the section on areas for improvement and asks for general comments and suggestions as to how the school should approach them. By far the largest number of comments come from parents interested in the way in which the school can improve its out of hours study support through the website, so the enquiry focus for the school is how to improve both the content and the uptake of the website. However, the school is concerned to keep all parents informed and on-side, so they send a letter home with a tear-off response sheet (below).

Thank you for your responses to our good Ofsted report, a credit to our staff and students. Most people have responded to the areas for improvement by saying that they'd like us to focus on the study support part of our website. We'll be working on all the areas highlighted by the inspectors but we'd like to know your top priorities, too. Please put '1' next to the most important and so on, down to '6' for the least important.

Lunchtime clubs	Study support on the website
Changing facilities in the gym	Mentor programme for Year 7s
Extended hours in the library and ICT areas	School garden

Figure 7.6 Example information sheet for parents

Potentially, they have missed a trick by not putting this sheet in with the Ofsted report itself but the reality is that you rarely think of these things at the time and they get a reasonable response rate of around 40%, which confirms that the website is the top priority, though changing rooms in the gym and extended hours for the library also score highly. Taking this into account, the research question begins to change, becoming about independent study and access to resources. The school designs a questionnaire for pupils about homework and independent study which asks about resources at home and the workload across the week in different subjects – this is filled in during Form group time and has a 98% response rate – and the analysis reveals that there are particular resource 'flashpoints' especially relating to GCSE coursework and resources. These results are shared with the parents through paper letters and the new parent webmail service, which sends emails to parents tailored to their child/ren's year group(s) and special interests. The letter asks for parent volunteers from the sixth form to come into a series of subject-specific focus groups discussing their experiences of coursework, and for volunteers from the GCSE years to become part of an advisory group to develop better resources. Parents from years 7 and 8 are invited to a series of open events in the day and evening to explore the current website and library provision alongside teaching assistants.

The school reports and open evenings in this school year have explicit feedback sheets and opportunities to informally canvass parents' opinions about the changes and the current provision. It becomes clear that there is a core group of active parents who have become very involved in the project and a larger group who are interested but who feel they cannot offer time or expertise. Of particular concern is a smaller group who feel that their resources do not stretch to providing technology at home and who are becoming increasingly worried that this is significantly disadvantaging their children.

At each stage, the project team within the school feed back information to the parents and this builds up parents' confidence that they have a voice. The extension of library and computer cluster hours to include Saturday morning access becomes a higher priority as a result of the open evening data, and funding is diverted to provide staffing. A mini-project to track the 'extended hours users' is initiated, with early self-report from students and homework feedback suggesting that it is of significant value.

Keeping your balance: consultation, collaboration and partnership

Earlier in this chapter we talked about the various approaches to research involving parents as if they were separate, or necessary stages in a linear process. Of course, over time, they begin to form themselves into an overlapping figure (7.7, below) where the findings from one kind of enquiry inform another, reflecting different priorities at different times in the research cycle.

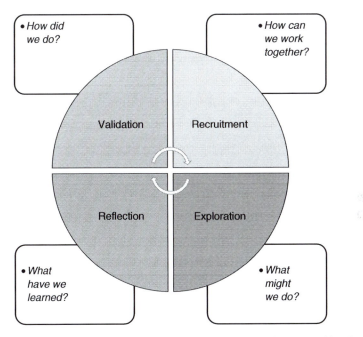

Figure 7.7   Model of consultation, collaboration and partnership in parental involvement

It is very difficult for teachers to balance the competing demands of students' immediate needs, curriculum change, assessment regimes and personal and professional development. Sometimes, working with parents can seem to be an additional demand on an already over-burdened profession: an area of risk (since few teachers have been trained to work with parents) and scant reward (since the development of effective home–school partnerships takes time. The need for close relationships to sustain home–school links is made harder by the reality that school populations are transient; the effort needs to be made anew with each cohort of students. Parent involvement is never 'sorted' and this can be a source of frustration for teachers and for schools.

Engaging with parents through enquiry, however, provides a joint task with an explicit outcome that aims to benefit students. This is motivation for teachers and parents alike and there are many attendant benefits from joint endeavour: the development of a shared language about learning; opportunities to discuss the priorities for students' learning and a sense that the learning experience can be tailored to meet the needs of the students currently in the classroom. Having a short-term goal like this is far more achievable than a vague desire to 'work more closely' or 'encourage parents to become more engaged', though it is possible to move towards both of those worthy aspirations.

Key perspectives on working with parents

While parental involvement continues to be an area of concern, discussion and engagement, there are multiple perspectives on the ways in which schools and parents can, do and should interact.

Crozier, G. and Reay, D. (2005) *Activating Participation: Parents and Teachers Working towards Partnership*. Stoke on Trent: Trentham Books.

Gewirtz, S., Ball, S.J. and Bowe, R. (1995) *Markets, Choice and Equity in Education*. Buckingham: Open University Press.

Tett, L. (2001) 'Parents as problems or parents as people? Parental involvement programmes, schools and adult educators', *International Journal of Lifelong Education*, 20(3): 188–198.

Todd, L. (2006) *Partnerships for Inclusive Education. A Critical Approach to Collaborative Working*. London: Routledge.

Wolfendale, S. (1992) *Empowering Parents & Teachers: Working for Children*. London: Cassell.

References used in this chapter

Desforges, C. and Abouchaar, A. (2003) *The Impact of Parental Involvement, Parental Support and Family Education on Pupil Achievements and Adjustment: A Literature Review*. London: Department for Education and Skills.

Harding, N. (2006) 'Ethnic and social class similarities and differences in mothers' beliefs about kindergarten preparation', *Race, Ethnicity and Education*, 9(2): 223–237.

Hattie, J. (2009) *Visible Learning: a Synthesis of Over 800 Meta-analyses Relating to Achievement*. London: Routledge.

HEFCE (2005) 'Young Participation in Higher Education', available for download from http://www.hefce.ac.uk/pubs/hefce/2005/05_03/.

Mirza, H.S. (2006) 'Race', gender and educational desire', *Race, Ethnicity and Education*, 9(2): 137–158.

Sacker, A., Schoon, I. and Bartley, M. (2002) 'Social inequality in educational achievement and psychological adjustment throughout childhood: magnitude and mechanisms', *Social Science and Medicine*, 22(5): 863–880.

8

MAKING SENSE OF IT, MAKING CONNECTIONS AND BRINGING IT TOGETHER

Chapter enquiry questions

- What has emerged from your enquiry?
- Who are the groups in your intended audience and what kinds of evidence do they need?
- How can your enquiry interest and influence other people?

Introduction

We have structured this book as if research was a fairly linear process, since a book that reflected the unpredictability of real life research would be difficult to read. However, we want to emphasise that research projects, however well planned, are messy entities: timescales slip, personnel change and research tools seldom elicit exactly the answers we intend. Often, unexpected findings, problems and new questions emerge out of the process of enquiry, not just in the period of reflection at the end of the cycle but during data collection or as we engage with new perspectives from other people's research.

The reality of work in schools and the additional commitment that an enquiry brings mean that you may well be collecting data over a fairly extended period and it is likely that you will be analysing some portions of data while you are still collecting other sources. This can be an advantage, since you will have the flexibility to collect additional information if something has not gone to plan or if the research tool you used didn't answer your question in the way you'd anticipated. It is important to accept a level of messiness in research so that you can continue your project but there is a balance to be struck: if the burning question that emerges during data collection will entail a significant additional effort – new methods, new data collection, lots more time – then it may be wiser to postpone answering that question until the next enquiry cycle.

Having accepted this potential messiness, there will come a point when you feel that you have collected all or most of your data and you will be mainly focused on analysis and the dissemination of the findings. This chapter will go through this process, exploring how to approach different types of data and deciding on analysis techniques.

What went according to plan?

What was easier?

What was more difficult?

What was predictable?

What was surprising?

What would you tell someone else about this?

Figure 8.1   Key questions for reviewing your research

It is important, however, at this stage before embracing the final stages of the research cycle to take some time to reflect on the process of the research, as well as the content of the results. The experience of research, drawn from your memory or your research diary is a vital part of your findings and there are key questions (as shown in Figure 8.1) that will help you to explore your action research process. We have talked (in Chapters 1 and 2) about rigour in research and one of the crucial elements of rigour is replicability: can someone else read or hear about your work and then go on to do a similar kind of study in their own setting? It is vital that you give details of the way in which you have worked (including the successes and failures), who you have worked with and the measures that you have used to gauge change. It is important that you communicate the experience to those who follow as well as the results of your research; they are arguably equally important.

What have you got?

To assess where you are and what you need to do next, it is useful if you can create a record of your data collection along the lines of Table 8.1 below. This is invaluable while you are writing up to remind you of how many questionnaires, how long a gap between pre- and post-tests and whether all your interviews came after the observations, or if there was some overlap. This table can be used to tell the story of your data collection.

Table 8.1   Reviewing your data

Kind of data	Details (number of participants, tools used)	Number of collections (dates)
School data: attendance, behaviour		
Attainment data		
Observations		
Questionnaires		
Interviews		
Audio/Video		
Other (including research diaries)		

It is also useful at this point to think about the successes and failures which chart any research project: how well did each of the research methods work? Did they measure what you expected or hoped? In other words, you need to think about the reliability and validity of each of the methods, to what extent the data collection tools collect the same data and produce the same findings over time and to what extent your tools measure what you intended. So for example with school or college data such as attendance records and standardised tests, you would expect that they would be very good in measuring the same thing over time (have high reliability) and yet unless your research question is explicitly about attendance or attainment in tests then the validity might be lower. It is not uncommon to see research in which better attendance is treated as if it was the same as greater intrinsic motivation to learn, which ignores the many extrinsic factors that encourage people to show up in the morning (social pressures, financial incentives, lack of a better option, etc.).

In another scenario, interviews with a group of learners are likely to be high in validity in that you are likely to select interview questions based on your research questions. However, in that the group of learners is unlikely to stay the same (they will get older, have different experiences or they will be replaced by a new class) then the reliability is lower. Your interview data is an excellent 'snapshot' of their views in that moment but you have to be wary of saying 'this is what they thought, still think and will think forever' or 'this is what all groups of learners of this type think'. This should not mean that you discard any of your evidence, particularly where you have used a range of data collection tools to complement or triangulate but it does means that you need to think critically about the warrant you can place on each set of results.

Approaching the analysis

The sections that follow in this chapter will address some of the different techniques and considerations that different kinds of data require. There are, however, key principles when analysing, which apply to all kinds of data.

You are trying to answer your key research questions. The enquiry process will have thrown up all kinds of new ideas and themes, but it is important not to get side-tracked. As you work through your data, have your question pinned up somewhere prominent to help you keep focused. Look for evidence that confirms or refutes your hypothesis, and put everything else in the 'interesting, but not for now' pile.

Keep an analysis log. Write down every question that you ask the data in your research diary as you go along. This seems time consuming in the short term but it is nothing to having to re-analyse all your interviews because you can't remember if you searched for a particular theme, or re-watching all your video looking for the interactions of a particular child. The analysis log is also a record of your developing thinking and is very useful in structuring your writing up.

Follow your hunches about themes. As you work through the data, you will start to get a sense of what is important in your project: ideas and evidence will start to form clusters. At first, they might not seem to amount to much but bear in mind that you know more about this enquiry than anyone and your hunches are likely to be based on evidence that you have noticed in passing. This is the time to examine your hunches: note them in your diary and start to record evidence under the headings you've generated. You can search for common words and phrases which relate to these themes and explore whether different kinds of evidence come together under headings (do your test results and your interviews both support the theme?) and so begin to build a picture of where your evidence is strong.

Be careful about finding what you're looking for. It is inevitable that an enquiry that looks for a particular change will find *some* evidence of that change. It is human nature to seize on the positive evidence and place it 'front and centre' in a research report and to give a less prominent position to the ambiguous or negative findings. It is therefore incredibly important to do lots of counting, **especially** in qualitative research. If you have two wonderful quotes from interviews supporting your argument in the write-up, they will be even more wonderful if you can report that they are representative of the twenty five positive statements given on this theme and that only four negative statements were made. The reader will not then suspect that you have just cherry-picked those two and ignored the rest.

Your conclusions will be stronger if you can validate them with others. Working collaboratively with colleagues and research participants is the best way to ensure that your interpretation of the data is reasonable and representative. There are a variety of ways that you can approach this: you can ask a colleague to watch a short piece of video or read part of an interview transcript, without telling him what your conclusions have been and simply ask him what seems to be interesting or important. You can feed back your analysis at an early stage to research participants, by reporting questionnaire results to parents or students and asking them to flesh out the headlines, or to challenge your assumptions. As a matter of good ethical practice, anything you write about others should be available to them for their comment at a draft stage. Not everyone will want to read or comment on your research but the opportunity to pick up on errors of fact or interpretation should be there. Your research conclusions will be so much stronger when backed up by the validation of your colleagues and your participants.

Data from your institution

You may well have made use of the masses of data relating to attendance, behaviour and attainment that is collected every day. You need to be clear about what the data is: if you are looking at behaviour monitoring data for a group of students you need to state what is being recorded, by whom and when. You need to decide if it is a fair comparison to look at behaviour referrals from different staff members – does everyone use the same criteria? If you are confident that they do, you can report and compare levels of referral without further comment. However, if you are not sure, you will need to report that these are *possible* indications of students' behaviour. At the first level, you need to do counts and to keep accurate records of the time-frame; you can then go on to do comparisons with other groups or other years. Depending on the data, you may be able to make statements about cohorts, classes or individuals. The level of analysis and reporting that you use is up to you and is dependent on your audience: the example below gives a description of the measurement used and several different approaches to analysis.

Secondary School Example

In order to judge the effectiveness of the project we looked at the numbers of students signed into the Late Book. Only students who are more than fifteen minutes late (i.e. arriving after 9am) sign the book, since at that time the only point of entrance is the main foyer and they sign the book on their way in.

(Continued)

(Continued)

Descriptive

During the project, 24 students were signed into the late book, fewer than we would normally expect.

Comparative

In the spring term of 2006, 48 students signed in late, whereas in spring 2007 only 24 signed in late.

Analytic

During the 'Don't Be Late' project, the number of children signing in late fell by 50% compared to the previous year (n=24 in 2007, 48 in 2006). The late-comers were more boys than girls (17/7 in 2007, 31/17 in 2006) and were more likely to be older.

Analytic (individual tracking)

During the 'Don't Be Late' project, the number of children signing in late fell by 50% compared to the previous year (n=24 in 2007, 48 in 2006). The late-comers were more boys than girls (17/7 in 2007, 31/17 in 2006) and were more likely to be older. Of those children signing in late in 2007, the majority (n=16) were from Years 10 and 11 and only one was from Year 7. With the exception of this Year 7 student, all the students signing in late in 2007 had been late in 2006.

Attainment data

When looking at attainment data it is hard not to get sucked in to the sort of mind-set which suggests that only a significant improvement in nationally standardised tests 'counts'. Within research, however, a range of measures are commonly used: teacher assessments, standardised tests and national assessments measure different outcomes. Some assessment measures require you to perform both pre- and post-tests, while others are 'norm-referenced' and allow you to use them once and then compare the results to scores matched to average performance by age. This is where your research question and your intent in the enquiry are crucial: you need to be clear about whether the kind of question you've asked matches the measure you've used and this affects the kinds of comparative statements you can make (see Table 8.2 below for some examples).

Table 8.2   Using your research question and intent to isolate your findings

Question	Measure	Comparison
How well can Jimmy do on Task A? (standardised)	Norm-referenced test of performance on Task A	Jimmy's score is above average for his age
Can Jimmy get better at Task A? (ipsative 1)	Pre- and post-test designed to measure performance on Task A	Jimmy improved his pre-test score by 10 points
Can Jimmy get better at Task A? (ipsative 2)	Ongoing teacher assessment	Jimmy's work shows development and improvement over time
Can performance in Task A be improved in this class? (cohort 1)	National test data (e.g. SATs, GCSEs)	Jimmy's class have scored higher than last year's group
Can performance in Task A be improved in this class? (cohort 2)	Pre- and post-test designed to measure performance on Task A	Jimmy's class have all improved their scores by between 3 and 14 points

You'll notice that none of the examples in the table above uses a contemporary control group – a matched group sitting the same assessment at the same time. Control groups are used less frequently in practitioner enquiry and some teachers feel that this makes their research less valid. We would argue that the question is not one of validity but of the kinds of claims you can make for the data: you can't use any of that data to make a direct causal link between the score Jimmy achieved and the intervention used by his teacher to effect change. You can speculate that the difference between pre- and post-testing might be connected to the intervention and you could also speculate that the difference between this cohort and the previous one was affected by the changes the teacher made, but you would need much more information about how similar that cohort was to Jimmy's class before you could make that claim with confidence. However, supposing that Jimmy's teacher was able to persuade her colleague in Year 6, who had a class from broadly similar backgrounds, with the same mix of ability levels, first language and other relevant factors to run pre- and post-tests of critical thinking with her students, without employing the critical thinking curriculum. This looks like a workable control group and differences between the scores can be looked at (see Table 8.3 below).

The obvious first implications of this data are that Jimmy's teacher has proved her hypothesis: a critical thinking intervention has shifted all her students' scores up – though the range suggests that the effect is variable and some children got more from it than others – and her class has done significantly better in the post-test than the control group, suggesting that they have done much better than they would have done without the intervention. However, it's important to look closely at the control group scores

Table 8.3   Example of using a control group as a comparison

	Number of students	Pre-test scores Average (range)	Post-test scores Average (range)
Jimmy's class	30	21 (13–32)	29 (17–44)
Control class	29	16 (11–24)	19 (13–29)

to make sure that we don't over-state the effect that Jimmy's teacher has had. The control group class score lower on the pre-test, too, suggesting that Jimmy's teacher has been infusing critical thinking skills in her teaching already (there's a reason she chose this intervention: it suits her beliefs and the way she likes to work with the children). Also, the control class make some progress over time, between 2 and 5 points at the top and bottom of the range (and you'd have to check for individual children in that group making greater leaps, or even going backwards; averages can hide a lot), so you'd have to subtract a small amount from the gains that Jimmy's class made to account for this. The reason for all this caution is the way in which research findings can be used: if you look at the headlines of this research, you might conclude that all the teachers in Jimmy's school should use the critical thinking intervention and that it would have a broadly equivalent effect on all the children. Our experience in the real world of learning and teaching suggests that this is not the case.

Observations, including audio and video

When you do an observation, you are analysing from the moment you begin. Before you even pick up a pencil, you have decided upon what to record, and what to ignore. The inherent slant in an observation makes the counting part of the analysis all the more important. Tally charts are a good place to start, based around the following questions: *who, what, when, with whom, how many, how often, how long* and as many others as you need to address your question.

Infant School Example

Moira was observing the use of the role play area as part of her enquiry into children's use of mathematical language in their play. These tally charts represent data from two periods of observations at each end of her project.

Who/How many	Early observations	Later observations
Anna	2	3
Ben	0	1
Charlie	4	3
Dawn	0	0
Eddie	3	5
Farah	2	2

With whom	Early observations	Later observations
Anna	Saira, Nadia	Saira, Helen
Ben		Eddie
Charlie	Nick	Nick
Eddie Tyrone, Josh, Philip	Ben, Tyrone, Farah	
Farah	Lucy, Josh	Eddie, Nadia

What/who	Early observations	Later observations
House (Chores)	Saira, Nadia	
House (relationships)	Farah, Lucy	Saira, Helen
Fantasy (task/adventure)	Tyrone, Josh, Philip, Lucy, Charlie, Nick	Ben, Tyrone, Farah, Charlie, Nick
Fantasy (relationships)	Anna, Saira	Anna, Helen

Often with observations, you will be comparing over time and one critical element here is to make sure that the description of the behaviour observed is accurate. This is important even when you are doing all the observations, as your focus may shift as the research progresses, but it is crucial if the observations are being done by others as well as you. Many hours spent in meetings debating what is meant by an open question or what constitutes off-task behaviour have convinced us that it is well worth having this clarified early, written down and adhered to. From your research diary, you will need to make clear how similar the occasions of repeat observations were to the first, what the differences were and what impact you judge these differences to have made, if any.

Once you have made the counts, you can explore the patterns which are emerging, some of which may be surprising. By basing your analysis of themes on the counts, you will be able to report accurately whether an observed incident is typical, part of a larger pattern of behaviour for a group or individual or unusual, yet significant. It is very important to distinguish between an observed behaviour which is typical of the other behaviours in your observations and one which only occurs infrequently in the observation but which you have often experienced in 'normal' classroom life. Your on-going experience with the students is data, but it is a different kind of data and must be reported differently from a structured observation.

For audio and video recordings, you need to follow a similar protocol with regard to counting, though by using these technologies, things like length of speech and non-verbal interactions become easier to explore. Video and audio are very data-rich, so choose short sections to analyse for your own sanity but be very clear to report if these are typical or unusual excerpts. Of course, permission is required from staff, pupils and parents to use visual images in reporting (see Chapter 5). Observations are particularly prone to interpretation by the observer, so a discussion with 'the observed' to validate your analysis is particularly helpful here. If you have used audio or video, you can play short sections and describe your interpretation, giving colleagues or students an opportunity to support or challenge your understanding.

Questionnaires

If you have used questionnaires the first task, which you can get started with before you get any back, is constructing your database. The best place to do this is in Excel, since it is easier to use than other statistical packages and has the facility to make graphs quickly and effectively. Using the first page of the questionnaire from Chapter 5 devised by Lanner School in Cornwall, a fictitious sample of results is given in the database (below).

<u>Lanner Parent Questionnaire</u>

<u>About your child's learning at school</u>

1. How confident are you that you know <u>what</u> your child is learning at school? *Please tick one box*

Not at all confident	I know some of what is going on	I know most of what is going on	Very confident

2. How do you find out <u>what</u> your child is learning at school? *Please tick all that apply*

The school send me letters and leaflets	My child tells me	My child's teacher tells me	I hear about things from other parents	Other (please state below)

Other ways of finding out _____

3. How confident are you that you understand how your child is learning at school? *Please tick one box*

Not at all confident	I know some of what is going on	I know most of what is going on	Very confident

4. How do you find out how your child is learning at school? *Please tick all that apply*

The school send me letters and leaflets	My child tells me	My child's teacher tells me	I hear about things from other parents	Other (please state below)

Other ways of finding out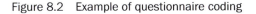

5. Would you be interested in finding out more about what and how your child is learning at school? *Please tick one box*

Yes	No

Responses are scored 1–4 for Q1 and Q3

Responses are scored 1–5 for Q2 and Q4

For Q5 Yes scores 1, No scores 0

Figure 8.2   Example of questionnaire coding

The teachers at Lanner asked a range of open and closed questions, so there are a variety of things that can be done with this data. For questions 1 and 3 there are some simple calculations that can be performed: by adding up the totals one can see that parents in this sample are more confident about *what* their children are learning than about *how* they are learning it.

Calculating the mean and standard deviation focuses attention on those few parents at the extremes of confidence, both high (Parents 5 and 10) and low (Parents 4 and 9), as atypical. Questions 2 and 4 ask for the source of information, which can be represented in another table (8.5, below), where it becomes clear that children themselves are the main source of information on the process of learning.

Table 8.4   Example of data including mean and standard deviation calculations

	Q1 Confident 'what'	Q2	Q2 Other	Q3 Confident 'how'	Q4	Q4 Other	Q5
Parent 1	3	1, 2, 4		2	2		1
Parent 2	3	2, 3		3	2, 3		1
Parent 3	2	2, 4		2	2, 4		1
Parent 4	1	5	No one tells me	1	5	I don't know who to ask	1
Parent 5	4	1, 3		4	1, 2, 3		0
Parent 6	2	1, 2		1	2		1
Parent 7	3	1, 2, 3		3	2, 3		1
Parent 8	2	1, 4		1	2, 4		1
Parent 9	1	2, 4		1	2		0
Parent 10	4	1, 2		3	2, 3		1
Total	25			21			8
Mean	2.5			2.1			
Standard Deviation	1.08			1.1			

Table 8.5   Example of data processing from other questions

	School	Child	Teacher	Parents	Other
Information on what	6	5	3	4	1
Information on how	1	9	4	2	1

At this point it becomes tempting to speculate: are there connections between where you get your information and how confident you are? Does the level of confidence impact on desire to get involved? Do other parents make you feel more or less confident? Some, though by no means all, of these questions are addressed by this data and speculative questions like these should be reported as 'areas for further investigation'.

Interviews

Interviews are at the same time the hardest and the most pleasurable things to analyse, because they are so rich and contain so much for you to engage with. Even using a very structured schedule, there will be all kinds of surprising and interesting themes which can emerge. So, back to your key research questions in order to keep on track. The transcript below is a section from a much longer interview with a teacher about his research.

The annotations represent the first level notes made in the analysis of this and the other interviews in this series, highlighting sections which relate to the principal object of the interviews – exploring research-active teachers' influence on their colleagues – noting key phrases and words which will be searched for throughout the data set. In addition, a particular phrase is highlighted. When we heard the words during the interview we became quite excited; this was exactly what we were looking for! It would even make a rather good journal article title. This is the 'seductive quote': the answer to a researcher's prayer and, more frequently than we'd like, our downfall. It is too easy to be dazzled by quotes like this and to give them undue prominence in your writing. Unfortunately for our phantom article, not enough of the other data from the interviews supported this to make it a fully fledged theme.

Elaine (researcher): Could you start with what you feel the most important changes have been as a result of this project?

Sections relevant to our research question: 'How do teachers engaged in research influence their colleagues?'

Bob (teacher): I think that the most important change has probably been getting the whole school learning rather than teaching. Is that sufficient or would you like me to go further?

Elaine: Yes please that sounds really interesting.

Bob: Well its there are lots of other things that I am trying to do at the moment, not least the KS 3 strategy and that kind of thing, which has come on the back of the research project work. The [funding body] started as a major influence in all of that. Me taking on research projects in the school has made my colleagues really **reflect** on why they are doing and why we're doing what we are doing as a school. I did a thing about the research, a whole staff inset evening about 3 months ago. I got some tremendous **feedback** from that, that made me understand what an impact it had. In my jaundiced moments I think 'Why am I doing this, why am I doing this?' but actually the feedback was fantastic and a lot of people saw the research project if nothing else acting as a '**conscience for the school**'. It is a phrase that I coined but other people bought into it, this idea that we otherwise bundle along doing stuff and not **reflecting** on why we are doing it.

Key words from the project to search for in this interview (and others)
Reflect (ing/ion)
Feedback

'Conscience for the school', fantastic quote!! (Beware...)

As you read and re-read your interviews (or listen and re-listen to audio recordings if you haven't transcribed them) you'll become aware of frequencies and trends in your data and will be able to build up themes, gathering together quotes and sections. However you do this, by cutting and pasting in Word, or snipping up copies of the interviews and putting them in folders, you must keep a record of how many individuals support a theme and how many times they support it. Bob's interview contains a great deal of material on the importance of staff meetings for the development of research culture but the seven quotes from him are not enough to emphasise this factor in the research report without the evidence that nine other teachers talked about it in their interviews as well. In reporting interview data you must say how many people mention something that you advance as evidence and how often: '*Most students were positive about the project*' is not nearly as strong as '*Seven out of the eight students interviewed had positive things to say about the project*. Commonly used terms were 'exciting' (n=6), 'fun' (n=12) and 'challenging' (n=5). The negative comments from the other students also related to challenge: '*I thought the whole thing was too hard for us; it felt like it had been designed for older kids*'.

As the example indicates, it is a good idea to highlight the contrasts in your data, the elements which challenge the majority view and your hypothesis. When asking people to be interviewed you offer them a platform to express their views, so you are ethically obliged to represent their views, even if you give greater weight to the views of others. So much of the analysis of interviews depends on your judgement, so it is important to validate your themes and to weave together the data from your interviews with data from other sources, such as observations and school or assessment data.

Communicating your findings

When you are thinking about the information to include in a report about your enquiry it is useful to contemplate one of three frames which can help to structure the process. Firstly it is useful to think of the things you as a teacher would need to know to persuade you to use a specific innovation in your own teaching: the school/classroom context, the demographics of the class, the organisation decisions that need to be made, the preparation involved and an honest appraisal of the successes and failures. In that you are likely to have an audience of teachers, it is important to keep their agendas in mind.

The second frame we would recommend is a structure that should be familiar as one recommended in Science from Key Stage 2 upwards, the experiment write-up: what you wanted to find out, what you did, how you did it, what your findings were and what this means to you. This structure will extend what could be a reflective lesson plan into the genre of research study, an investigation.

The third frame, and arguably the most important, is the action research frame: it is important to remember that your report is part of a process; you are at the 'making it public stage' of one cycle but you will be quickly moving forward into the next cycle of enquiry. This means there needs to be an aspect of your write-up which looks forward, appraising the lessons learned about teaching processes and research methods and the implications for school, teachers, pupils and parents, but also the implications for your own research focus – where will you be heading next: what is the next hunch you would like to explore and what are the links and learning which have got you there? The latter element is particularly important if findings have not been what you hoped or expected; there can still be some positive learning which can be achieved and the research can move on to address the issues. This can be seen in the quote below.

> In Year One of the research our findings were extremely positive with a positive effect size of 0.76 for peer assessment of writing; in other words an average class using this approach would move up from 50th to 23rd in a ranked list of 100 classes. However, in the second year of the research the findings were not as positive and although we learned from the conclusions and the school was able to move forward, the actual writing up was difficult in that we did not feel we had much positive to say. (Primary School)

Included in Figure 8.3 on the next page are some of the headings used by teachers in the Learning to Learn project to support the writing up process. In this project the teachers completed a written report which was available for download on the Campaign for Learning's website. This meant the audience was very open, including teachers, teacher educators, policy makers, parents and anyone interested in learning who googled their way to the site. This meant that the reports had to try to be comprehensive, clear and accessible. Hopefully there are elements from all three frames above apparent in the headings. We do not advocate that you need to use all or any of these specific headings, but they should provide a useful starting point from which you can devise your own structure. In blue, under each of the headings on the next page, there is also some guidance as to what could be included under each section. As before this is meant as a starting point and is by no means meant as a definitive list.

Context:
The school/ college:
Year groups involved
Details of school catchment
Statistics such as school roll, % SEN,
% EAL and % FSM
How involved in the project
Background of school in relation to
educational research
How this enquiry fits within the overall
development of the institution

The teacher(s):
Background in school and in teaching,
including relevant interests and research
Curriculum and development interests
Influences
Interest in project: benefits and challenges

The learners:
Focus year group/class and why
number in class/year group
% SEN etc.
Characteristics e.g. lively, inquisitive
Targets and achievements while in school

The Project:
Rationale:
Reasons for involvement in project
Why this area
Need of the learners
Relate to interests and background

Objectives:
Subject area
Key objectives
Target learners

Hypothesis:
Written in the form of a question

Research Process:
Teachers' choices:
How the teacher(s) chose to tackle the
project aims
Which strategies were chosen and why
Detail about how the strategies were
implemented in the classroom
Reaction towards the research process
and the choice of method

Evidence collected:
Data collected to record whether aims
achieved

Reasons for choosing different methods
of data collection
Strengths and weaknesses of the tools
chosen

Discussion of Results:
Findings:
Whether your findings have achieved your
initial aims
Evidence in support of and against your
hypothesis
Interesting aspects of the process
Unexpected effects
Benefits to pupils
Benefits for the teacher(s)
Negative effects for teacher(s) and pupils
Evidence from pupil/teacher/parent
quotes included here
Evidence in the form of digital images can
also be included here

Extensions and changes to method:
Did you change anything while the project
progressed?
Why?
What were the effects of this?
What did you do extra?
Why?
Influence on the project

Conclusions:
Developing this approach:
If you used this process again what would
you keep the same?
What would you make different?
Why?
Any adaptations to the strategies used?
How would it work on a larger scale?
How would it work with other age ranges?
Changes to strategies used
School developments as a
consequence
Teacher developments as a
consequence
Pupil developments as a consequence

Summary:
3 most important impacts/findings of the
project
How the teacher(s) felt about the project
as a whole
Impact on institution
Impact on teacher
Impact on learners

Figure 8.3   Exemplar structure for writing up

There are always worries from practitioners writing about their enquiries that this is not 'proper' research and, indeed, some academics consider the work produced by practising teachers to be a 'different' kind of knowledge. There is a way round this but it is not an easy option. In Chapter 3 we looked at the criteria we use to judge the quality of an academic article or a research report (Table 8.6 below); the challenge now is to apply these criteria to our own writing.

Table 8.6   Research checklist

Key questions	✓
Who took part in this study?	
Are details given of age, gender, ability, special needs, socio-economic status, ethnicity and culture?	
Are details given of how they were recruited, what ethical steps were taken and who dropped out?	
Were the participants in their normal setting, working with their usual teacher?	
What outcomes were investigated?	
Was the focus on	

- attainment (knowledge, skills, understanding),
- attitude (to the content, to the process, to the self as learner),
- behaviour (increase in positive or decrease in negative),
- or a combination?

How were the outcomes measured?	
Who designed the measures?	
If there were questionnaires, interviews or observations, were the instruments included for you to see?	
If there was an intervention, was there 'before' and 'after' data?	
If views were gathered, was the sample large and representative enough?	
How was the data analysed?	

- If it's numbers, does it state which tests were used and give you enough detail to check it?
- If it's words, does it explain how the themes were generated and how the words were placed within the themes?

As for others' work, we don't judge a practitioner enquiry as if it was a randomised control trial or a longitudinal cohort study over 30 years. We take the standards for a 'good enough' enquiry as set out throughout this book and apply those. If you write clearly about how your enquiry came about, about the questions you asked and the tools you chose to answer them then your enquiry can stand alongside other research without embarrassment. After all,

It is the teachers who will change the world of the school by understanding it. (Halsey, 1972: 165)

References used in this chapter

Halsey, A.H. (ed.) (1972) *Educational Priority. IEPA Problems and Policies.* Report of a research project sponsored by the Department of Education and Science and the Social Science Research Council. London: HMSO quoted in L. Stenhouse, (1975) *An Introduction to Curriculum Research and Development.* London: Heinemann: 208.

9

SHARING YOUR FINDINGS, FINDING NEW QUESTIONS

Chapter enquiry questions

- Who needs to know about my enquiry?
- How can I share my findings?

'Teacher-researchers need to present their findings – this is a priority'. (Teacher-researcher, Leading Edge Action Research Partnership School)

Who needs to know about my enquiry?

In Chapter 1 we explained the principles underpinning our work in partnership with teachers and our debt to the work of Lawrence Stenhouse, who said that practitioner research should be 'systematic enquiry made public', but there has been debate as to what exactly 'making your enquiry public' might mean. In the first instance, sharing your findings is important for your own learning as it helps you to articulate and clarify your thoughts. Using personal experience in order to engage with a problem and construct a theory develops a critical capacity and an understanding of uncertainty that strengthens professional judgement and facilitates the management of change.

It is also important for colleagues not directly involved to hear about what you have been doing. Your findings can contribute to the promotion of professional dialogue within your school by posing problems, highlighting issues and outlining possible solutions based on real situations. The teachers we have worked with comment on how discussion of their findings leads them to realise new things about routine behaviour in the classroom.

Enquiry and evidence-based decision making is the key to internal capacity building in schools through sustaining the continuous learning of teachers by building on their interest in enhancing pupil learning. The gathering of concrete data in context means that processes of review and the management of change can be more effective. Practitioner enquiry can support the implementation of new ideas and practices in school by encouraging reluctant

... [I] look at initiatives in a different way, am more analytical about what will work for the child and feel open to new ways of learning and new methods of teaching. Trying new initiatives, trialling them, evaluating them and either putting them into practice or discarding them is not so daunting now. (Primary School)

... for the first time teachers were asking, 'What do you and Lynn do in the rainbow room?', and they asked to have a staff meeting about it. (Primary School)

... we had never really discussed why we record in different ways. We had never reflected on why on some days we do not do any recording ... This made us stop and think. (Primary School)

colleagues to have a go and try new ideas persuaded by the evidence of tangible benefits for pupils. As can be seen in one of the schools above, the presence of enthusiasts in the staffroom who are excited about what they are learning can create interest in finding out what is going on.

Creating interest in your findings is usually most effective when there is emphasis on the context in which you work and the processes you used in your enquiry but it is these features that can sometimes make it difficult to explain what you have done to a wider audience. Conventional methods of publicising the outcomes of research that are used in the educational research community are not particularly useful for the sharing of this rich, localised knowledge. The importance of face-to-face contact through networks of practitioners has been highlighted as a key feature of effective dissemination (McLaughlin and Black-Hawkins, 2007) and is supported by the experience of the teachers with whom we have worked. Recent thinking on the nature of the 'public' who need to be informed of the outcomes of teacher research has tended to favour more organic, dynamic networks of interested colleagues (Posch, 1994) so that ideas are first made public to the village rather than to the world. According to this model of dissemination, it is the encouragement to replicate ideas by trying them out for yourself that is important and for this to happen, personal experience, shared interests and transparent accounts of processes are essential.

In this way, teacher enquiry offers a new perspective on research by empha-sising the importance of the knower as well as the status of the knowledge:

> ... it is not enough that teachers' work should be studied: they need to study it for themselves. What we need is a different view of research which begins with our own work and which is founded in curiosity and a desire to under-stand; which is stable, not fleeting, systematic in the sense of being sustained by a strategy. (Stenhouse, 1985: 1)

How can I share my findings?

The teachers with whom we have worked have used a variety of ways of sharing their enquiries with colleagues. Sometimes the dissemination has been within the institution, at least at first, while others have made use of networks to share their work across professional communities.

Table 9.1   Methods for sharing practitioner enquiry

Posters	Visual displays of an enquiry on a colourful poster using headings such as 'What? When? Why? How?' to summarise the key points.	Within the institution
'Show and Tell' lunches	The Senior Management team provide a small budget to pay for a free lunch once a month and teachers meet to share ideas, swap resources, and discuss findings.	Within the institution
Item on the agenda of staff meetings	Including an update on practitioner enquiry in the agenda for meetings shows that it is a priority and helps to remind all staff of what is happening.	Within the institution
Including a section on practitioner enquiry in the staff handbook	Set an expectation of teachers as researchers as an integral part of the school/department culture. Include examples of research tools and sample case studies.	Within the institution
Set up a space for sharing ideas/ resources on the school/college/ department intranet	This can be useful but needs to be linked to other forms of dissemination as people tend to need prompting to consult a website.	Within the institution
Peer observation and coaching	Time is given to staff to pair up and observe each other while trying out a new strategy with a class/ group. The feedback can help in refining the strategy and also serve as a source of data in a case study. It is important to maintain a distinction between this kind of collaborative working and performance management.	Within the institution Across institutions

(Continued)

Table 9.1 (Continued)

Small grants for projects	Setting up a bidding process for funding for projects to build on the outcomes of previous enquiries.	Within the institution Across institutions
Learning Walks	Exchange visits by staff, or students, in which the host outlines a particular project/initiative and the visitors look for evidence of impact. The important element of a Learning Walk is the discussion of what has been seen and how this is interpreted. Comparing the different perspectives can often be the stimulus for a new enquiry.	Across institutions
CPD conferences	Workshops presented by teachers have a powerful effect as they are grounded in shared everyday experiences of teaching and learning.	Across institutions

We can identify some common characteristics within the different ways of sharing the findings from practitioner enquiries that have been developed by our colleagues in schools, colleges and universities.

Production of practical, tangible artefacts

Teachers need something that they can apply and test out in their own context. This is consistent with what we know about the use of practical tools to structure participation and further understanding of practice within a community (Bielaczyc and Collins, 1999). Teachers will often talk about 'stealing' good ideas from colleagues and the artefacts can be a means of building on this tendency to promote the dissemination of research.

Transparency in the sharing of processes as well as outcomes

We have already emphasised the importance of making any reporting of an enquiry transparent as part of the means of ensuring the rigour of your research. Colleagues also need to know how any tools have been developed and used in order to have the capacity to make best use of them and adapt and innovate.

Encouraging replication

Presenting your findings in forms that can be used, but which also make the processes of their production and use clear, invites colleagues to replicate what you have done. By applying the outcomes of your enquiry in a new context they will be able to either validate them or pose new questions (often they will do both at the same time). The invitation is, in the spirit of collaborative enquiry, to 'try this for yourselves; this is what I did and this is what I found. What do you think?'

Creating structures of support

In our experience, the best support occurs through encouraging organic growth as is expressed succinctly by one Teacher-researcher:

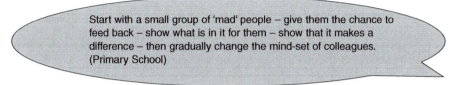

Start with a small group of 'mad' people – give them the chance to feed back – show what is in it for them – show that it makes a difference – then gradually change the mind-set of colleagues. (Primary School)

It requires the bringing together of top-down and bottom-up support so that the enthusiasts are given scope to develop their ideas within a managed system that provides encouragement, recognition and resources.

Widening participation

Gradually widening the circle of who is involved enables different perspectives to emerge. Including teachers from other institutions, learners as student researchers, parents and the local community can drive forward interlocking cycles of enquiry, as in the secondary and primary schools quoted below:

The research projects are regularly shared with colleagues, pupils and parents through a variety of media and the school has a 'research culture' which lies at the heart of decision-making in school. Cross-curricular working groups both consult research projects and do their own, as policies are reviewed or created. (Secondary School)

It gave us a sense that we were not alone in any difficulties we were having and it was also great to share successes and new ideas. (Primary School)

The teachers we have worked with have valued the opportunity to be part of a wider network that helped to develop social relationships and enabled experiences to be shared. The importance of encouraging positive social relationships for the creation of knowledge was highlighted in a recent study of school–university partnerships in the Netherlands and the US:

> Schools with well-connected networks, where ideas, knowledge and resources are exchanged with a high number of colleagues across the network, provide contexts that foster knowledge processes. School structures and activities need to deliberately foster such connectivity between colleagues by providing a range of on-going opportunities to interact, collaborate and exchange with colleagues inside as well as outside their own groups in school ... (Cornelissen, 2011: 197)

Networks are also important in the uptake of research evidence as building relationships and sharing the conduct and analysis of research increases confidence and this is as important as knowing about research techniques or evidence (Simons et al., 2003).

The experiences of teachers attending the annual Learning to Learn (L2L) residential event demonstrate the potential of networks of practitioners engaged in enquiry to cross the boundaries between educational contexts. The first residential involved primary and secondary teachers working in cross-phase groups. Any initial apprehensions about the feasibility of sharing experiences were quickly dispelled as participants discussed strategies for improving learning. As the network expanded, participants in subsequent years included lecturers in FE colleges and from higher education. In each case practitioners across the phases of education were able to find common interest and valued the opportunity to learn from each other. At the final residential we asked the participants to identify the Plus, Minus and Interesting points of belonging to the network and this is a summary of their responses (Table 9.1).

Table 9.2   Exploring the learning in a practitioner enquiry network

Plus points	+	Developing a common educational identity through shared problems, shared solutions and a shared community
	+	Re-energising enthusiasm for learning by seeing things from different perspectives
	+	Discovering new ways of doing things and picking up useful ideas
	+	Understanding the learner across the phases of their educational experience
	+	Crossing the boundaries between the different phases of education encourages more abstract thinking about educational issues
	+	Permission to think 'big thoughts'

Minus points	–	There is a risk of being too general and superficial
	–	Jargon specific to each context can obscure meaning
	–	Developing an understanding of different contexts is time consuming
	–	Not everything about a particular project is relevant
	–	Need to be more rigorous about what is salient within the accounts of different experiences
Interesting points	?	The breadth of questions being asked in the enquiries is thought provoking
	?	The opportunity to expand your 'teacher speak' vocabulary
	?	Finding ways to share ideas more often

Teachers sometimes lack confidence in the status and credibility of their research and can be reluctant to share their findings. They worry that their enquiries are small in scale and too closely linked to their own concerns. Making your enquiry public is particularly difficult when the outcomes are not positive. Although knowing what hasn't worked is important, sharing this can be a challenging process.

> Overall we have found the research useful, but the difficulty of making public and personally dealing with, after a great deal of hard work, neutral or negative findings should not be underestimated. (Primary School)

While it may not always be possible to present this new learning in a polished form, it is still significant. Charting the move from a belief or a 'hunch' about an issue to collecting evidence and formulating an interpretation of the outcome is vital and it is the fact that it is specific to a particular context that makes it so valuable. The process of enquiry is an important part of dealing with the messy and ill-structured problems we face in the daily practice of the classroom. We need personal accounts from people with direct experience of classrooms because these can be the most persuasive:

> Authentic stories of learning and leadership need to be told through the voice of those who lived the stories (Krovetz and Arriaza, 2006).

There has been criticism of the tendency for teacher-researchers not to link their enquiries to existing research and so risk 're-inventing the wheel'. We find that if teachers begin with investigating their own questions directly in an enquiry this will lead them at a later stage to look beyond their own experience and to take account of what other people may have said about an issue. We have described this as a process of beginning with engaging *in* research as the stimulus for engaging *with* research (Baumfield et al., 2007). Teacher enquiry can enhance the relevance of existing research and also build research capacity within the profession.

Promoting partnerships between schools and university researchers can facilitate the use of a wider range of sources of evidence in the process of enquiry. In Sweden there is a policy for school improvement through the combining of curriculum and teacher development through action research projects facilitated by university researchers. They have found that initially teachers relied upon individual experience rather than literature or existing research. They also found that co-operation between teachers was rare and the dissemination of ideas and results meagre. After the 3 year development project working in partnership with the university, there was more teacher co-operation and dialogue in school about pedagogy, leading to a desire for further knowledge (Rosendahl and Ronnerman, 2006). Making links with existing research through this kind of partnership can overcome the problem that in many cases teachers do not engage with research because even when they are able to physically access sources (and this can be very difficult if you are not a member of academic staff or a student at a university) they find the kind of knowledge they provide does not meet their needs. Collaborative research partnerships encourage different perspectives and expertise to be employed to achieve a shared purpose. They can subvert a theory and practise division that makes the translation of knowledge from one context to another very difficult:

> ... because teachers and researchers work in unconnected problem spaces – even when the problems they are working on have the same name – teachers and researchers need to work together in tackling unsolved problems that are of central importance to teaching with enquiry acting as the common driver. Modern teachers need to be simultaneously active in two knowledge building communities; with their students building an understanding of the world and with researchers and other practitioners building a working knowledge of teaching and learning. (Bereiter, 2002: 416)

One question still to be answered is how important is it to have a written account of your enquiry? Some people see writing as an essential component of enquiry (Kelly, 2006) whereas for others it is adding an unnecessary burden to an already heavy workload. We have always encouraged teachers to aim for a written report of their research. We think the act of writing helps to make the process of the enquiry more explicit and the report itself can be a practical, tangible artefact productive of further learning. We argue that the requirement to write is a way of developing teacher autonomy through a shared understanding of the expectations of the craft of research (Ecclestone, 2004). Other commentators on the process of teacher research also support the view that writing is an important stage in the enquiry cycle (Rickert, 1991; Somekh, 2006). However, there has recently been some discussion of what exactly it might mean for a Teacher-researcher to make their enquiry public as advocated by Stenhouse. It has been suggested that it may be more appropriate in some instances to experiment with non-published forms of outcome or by publishing to the village rather than to the world (McIntyre, 2005). The reluctance of many teachers to produce formal, written outcomes from their enquiries has been noted in a number of otherwise successful teacher research projects such as the Teacher Training Agency's School-Based Research Consortia (Cordingley et al., 2002). The requirement to produce written reports of an enquiry certainly needs to be thought about carefully (like in the school example below) given the demands it can make on the teachers concerned and the risk of undesirable side-effects.

> ... negative effects for the teachers (and pupils) were that the school dramatically underestimated the amount of time needed to evaluate and write up the project. (Primary School)

It should also be recognised that producing a written account may make different kinds of demands on participants:

> ... deciding what to disclose and what to obscure or omit entails very different risks and consequences for the differently positioned writers in the group. (Cochran-Smith and Lytle, 2004: 641)

When considering the dissemination process it is worth going back to the selection of the target audience as part of your research design. We have discussed this earlier in the book in the context of a strategy for choosing data collection tools but it can also be used to decide how to share your findings. You will need to think about the opportunities you have and which of those you think will be most suitable. What is important about the communication of any findings is that it should demonstrate fitness for purpose. In what way do the outcomes from your enquiry provide a sufficient basis, a warrant, for future action? Decisions about the method of representing what you have learned should be made in order to enable other teachers to participate and apply their skills to the solving of a problem. We know that it can be difficult to involve colleagues who have not had the experience of being part of an enquiry and this is an issue for the scaling up of any initiative within a school. This can be seen in one of the examples below.

The teachers who took on the original focus groups … all had training in L2L and were enthusiastic about the benefits they could foresee. However, other teachers had to work out the advantages for themselves – after some persuasion from the original teachers – and, although all but one are keen and enjoying their teaching, it is a lesson to learn for the future. (Secondary School)

I am intrigued with the idea of schools being research schools as many staff develop interesting teaching and learning initiatives that with some research would show how their idea is effective. (Infant School)

The central concern regarding the sharing of findings with a 'public' should be to support the persuasive powers of the advocates of the enquiry and to interest the wider school community. How large a part writing up the enquiry plays, or what form it should take, is a decision to be made in terms of your intention, audience and its fitness for purpose.

Involvement in the research process gives teachers permission to look closely at the previous methods used and trial new ways of doing things. The findings at the end of each cycle not only justify doing this but also prompt more changes to occur. Parity between teachers and academics in research is achieved through the testing of ideas in the classroom and this is certainly the view of the teachers with whom we have worked.

Researchers working in the USA who have a great deal of experience of working with teacher-researchers identify three different enquiry–knowledge–practice relationships (Cochran-Smith and Lytle, 2004):

- Knowledge *for* practice – to implement/codify for dissemination (formal knowledge)
- Knowledge *in* practice – to uncover and enhance (situated knowledge)
- Knowledge *of* practice – to generate local knowledge within enquiry communities (testing knowledge in context)

Schools involved in systematic enquiry into the processes of teaching and learning foster all three forms of knowledge creation and can make a significant contribution to debate within the wider professional and academic community. Stenhouse used an analogy between aeronautical engineering and education to highlight the importance of practical, contextualised research for professional development and school improvement:

> ... to do research into building an aeroplane you have to build an aeroplane and not run along the tarmac flapping your arms – likewise, to do research into teaching you need to create some sort of instrument to research teaching. (Stenhouse, 1995: 59)

We know that managing schools as research cultures requires careful attention to the securing of adequate support and planning for varying degrees of involvement from staff at different points in the school year and at different times in an individual's career. If development is to be sustainable then a model accommodating waves of involvement attuned to the rhythm of life in the school has been found to be effective (Temperley and McGrane, 2005). John Dewey, an advocate of the value of teacher enquiry, talked of the need for 'critical optimism' (Shields, 2003) in order to manage the uncertainty and disappointment that can occur. It is important to be working within an environment where problem-posing as well as problem-solving is valued and in which encouragement to experiment also recognises that not everything will necessarily succeed. We know that enquiry into practice through action research has the potential to promote professional development and make a real difference to the lives of teachers and pupils in schools. It is fitting to leave the last word on this to a pupil in one of the schools:

> You can change things if you research well enough. (Student researcher, Leading Edge Action Research Partnership School)

Key readings and References

Ball, D.L. and Cohen, D.K. (1999) 'Developing practice, developing practitioners: toward a practice-based theory of professional education', in D. Sykes, and L. Darling-Hammond, (eds), *Teaching as the Learning Profession: Handbook of Policy and Practice*. San Francisco: Jossey-Bass, 3–32.

Baumfield, V., Hall, E., Higgins, S. and Wall, K. (2007) *Tools for inquiry and the role of feedback in teachers' learning*. Paper presented at the European Association of Research into Learning and Instruction (EARLI) Conference, Budapest, September 2007.

Bereiter, C. (2002) *Education and Mind in the Knowledge Age*. Mahwah, NJ: Lawrence Erlbaum Assoc.

Bielaczyc, K. and Collins, A. (1999) 'Learning Communities in Classrooms: a reconceptualization of educational practice', in C.M. Reigeluth, (ed.), *Instructional-Design Theories and Models: a New Paradigm of Instructional Theory*. Mahwah, NJ: Lawrence Erlbaum, 269–92.

Cochran-Smith, M. and Lytle, S. L. (2004) 'Practitioner Inquiry, Knowledge and University Culture', in J.J. Loughran, M.L. Hamilton, V.K. LaBoskey and T.L. Russell (eds), *International Handbook of Self-Study of Teaching and Teacher Education Practices.* Dordrecht: Kluwer Academic Publishers.

Cordingley, P., Baumfield, V.M., Butterworth, M., McNamara, O. and Elkins, T. (2002) *Lessons from the School-Based Research Consortia.* British Education Research Association: University of Exeter.

Cornelissen, F. (2011) *Knowledge Processes in School–University Research Networks.* Eindhoven: Eindhoven University of Technology.

Ecclestone, K. (2004) 'Learning in a comfort zone: cultural and social capital inside an outcome-based assessment regime', *Assessment in Education: Principles, Policy and Practice,* 11(1): 29–47.

Kelly, P. (2006) 'What is teacher learning? A socio-cultural perspective', *Oxford Review of Education,* 32(4): 505–19.

Krovetz, M.L. and Arriaza, G. (2006) *Collaborative Teacher Leadership: How Teachers Can Foster Equitable Schools.* Thousand Oaks, CA: Corwin Press.

Lave, J. and Wenger, E. (1991) *Situated learning: legitimate peripheral participation.* Cambridge: Cambridge University Press.

McIntyre, D. (2005) 'Bridging the gap between research and practice', *Cambridge Journal of Education,* 35(3): 357–82.

McLaughlin, C. and Black-Hawkins, K. (2007) 'School–university partnerships for educational research: distinctions, dilemmas and challenges', *Curriculum Journal* 18(3): 327–341.

Moon, J.A. (2004) *Reflection in Learning and Professional Development.* London: Routledge Falmer.

Posch, P. (1994) 'Networking in environmental education', in B. Pettigrew (ed.), *Evaluation and Innovation in Environmental Education.* Paris: OECD.

Rickert, A.E. (1991) 'Using teacher cases for reflection and enhanced understanding', in A. Lieberman and L. Miller (eds), *Staff Development for Education in the 90s,* New York: Teachers College Press: 112–32.

Rosendahl, L. and Ronnerman, K. (2006) 'Facilitating school improvement: the problematic relationship between researchers and practitioners', *Journal of In-service Education,* 32(4): 499–511.

Shields, P.M. (2003) 'The Community of Inquiry: classical pragmatism and public administration', *Administration and Society,* 35(5): 510–38.

Simons, H., Kushner, S., Jones, K. and James, D. (2003) 'From evidence-based practice to practice-based evidence: the idea of situated generalisation', *Research Papers in Education* 18(4): 347–64.

Somekh, B. (2006) 'Constructing intercultural knowledge and understanding through collaborative action research', *Teachers and Teaching: Theory and Practice,* 12(1): 87–106.

Stenhouse, L. (1981) 'What counts as research?', *British Journal of Educational Studies,* 29(2): 103–14.

Stenhouse, L. (1985) 'Action Research and the teacher's responsibility for the educational process', in J. Ruddock, and D. Hopkins (eds), *Research as a Basis for Teaching: Readings from the Work of Lawrence Stenhouse.* London: Falmer Press.

Temperley, J. and McGrane, J. (2005) 'Enquiry in Action', in H. Street and J. Temperley, (eds), *Improving Schools Through Collaborative Enquiry.* London: Continuum: 72–103.

INDEX